Rave

RAVE
YOUNG ADULT DRAMA

BLIZZARD PUBLISHING
Winnipeg • Niagara Falls

First published 2000 in Canada and the United States by
Blizzard Publishing Inc.
73 Furby Street, Winnipeg, Canada R3C 2A2.

Distributed in the United States by General Distribution Services,
4500 Witmer Industrial Estates, Niagara Falls, NY 14305-1386.

Cover art by Robert Pasternak.
Cover design by Otium.
Printed for Blizzard Publishing in Canada.

5   4   3   2   1

Blizzard Publishing gratefully acknowledges the support of
the Manitoba Arts Council, the Canada Council for the Arts, and
the Government of Canada through the Book Publishing Industry
Development Program for our publishing program.

Cataloguing in Publication Data

Rave, young adult drama.
    Contents: The other side of the closet / by Edward Roy — The face
is the place / by Beth Goobie — Chile con carne / by Carmen
Aguirre.
    ISBN 0-921368-95-X

1. Canadian drama (English)—20th century.* I. Roy, Ed. Other side of
the closet. II. Goobie, Beth, 1959–   . Face is the place. III. Aguirre,
Carmen, 1967–   . Chile con carne.

PS8315.R384 2000   C812'.608   C00–920020–7
PR9196.7.Y67R39 2000

Contents

THE OTHER SIDE OF THE CLOSET

BY
EDWARD ROY

The Other Side of the Closet was originally produced by Young People's Theatre of Toronto in collaboration with Youtheatre of Montréal in November 1997, with the following cast:

CARL	John Gordon
RICK	Peter Henein
TARA / RACHEL	M.J. Kang
PAULETTE	Corrinne Murray
JUSTIN / ANTONY	Jamie Robinson

Directed by Michel Lefebvre
Designed by Simon Guilbault
Original music and sound by Cathy Nosaty
Lighting designed by Steve Lucas
Stage Manager: Marinda deBeer

The Other Side of the Closet won a Dora Award for Outstanding Production. It was also nominated for a Chalmers Award.

Characters

CARL, 16

RICK, 16

JUSTIN, 15

ANTONY,
played by the same actor who plays JUSTIN

PAULETTE, 15

TARA, 16

RACHEL,
played by the same actor who plays TARA

Voice-overs:
MARION, Carl's mother
FRANK, Carl's father
Hot Line volunteers
various student voices

Setting

A city. The present.

Note

At times characters' lines overlap. Where this occurs, the point at which a line is overlapped by the one following is marked with "/".

Scene One

(On the street. The sound of city traffic is heard. RICK, JUSTIN, and CARL enter.)

CARL: Faggot!

RICK: Hey you! What are you looking at?

JUSTIN: Yeah, he's talking to you, queer ball.

CARL: Look at him just standing there.

RICK: Probably wants us to go over and give him a kiss.

JUSTIN: Kiss this, faggot!

CARL: Is this what you want, faggot?!

RICK: Come on, let's get him before he takes off.

JUSTIN: Yeah, run faggot run!

CARL: Faggot!

RICK: Pervert!

JUSTIN: Pig!

CARL, JUSTIN, and RICK: *(Together.) Faggot, pervert, pig!! Faggot, pervert, pig!! Faggot, pervert, pig!! Faggot, pervert, pig!!*

RICK: Kick him in the head! Kick him!

CARL: How do you like that, faggot?

JUSTIN: Oh, the fairy's crying.

RICK: Freak.

CARL: Come on guys, that's enough.

RICK: One more for luck.

JUSTIN: Let's go before someone calls the cops.

CARL: Rick, that's enough.

RICK: Just giving the faggot what he deserves. Let's go! Yeeeha!

(The boys run off as the sound of car horns in a traffic jam blare.)

Scene Two

(On the street. PAULETTE and TARA enter.)

TARA: Where the hell are they?

PAULETTE: Did you really expect them to be on time?

TARA: What if they don't show up?

PAULETTE: We'll go without them.

(CARL, JUSTIN, and RICK enter.)

JUSTIN: That was too much, man. Did you see his face when we caught him?

CARL: He was so scared he probably crapped his pants.

PAULETTE: Look who finally made it.

TARA: What took you guys?

RICK: We had some important business we had to take care of.

PAULETTE: More like you had to wait until somebody finished doing the dishes before mommy would let them out of the house.

JUSTIN: More like we had to take care of the trash.

(The guys laugh.)

RICK: Whoa, check that one out.

JUSTIN: Man, that is one ugly woman.

CARL: That's not a woman, dummy.

RICK: It's a faggot!

PAULETTE: Rick …

TARA: Ewww! I wouldn't be caught dead in that outfit.

CARL: Hey faggot, what are you hiding under that dress?

PAULETTE: Leave him alone.

RICK: It's sick, man.

PAULETTE: It's none of our business.

JUSTIN: It's just too freaky.

PAULETTE: What is?

CARL: Guys wearing dresses …

JUSTIN: And having sex with other guys.

RICK: Faggots!

PAULETTE: Will you please stop that? It's embarrassing.

TARA: God, I saw these two guys kissing in a movie and I was really grossed out—yuck—

RICK: Know what I'd do if one ever came on to me?

RICK, CARL, and JUSTIN: *(Together.)* Crunch him!

PAULETTE: Did we come downtown to see a concert or watch you guys act like jerks?

RICK: What's got into you?

PAULETTE: You're all acting like idiots over something you don't know anything about.

RICK: Oh yeah? What if a girl came on to you? Would you like that—

TARA: Ewww!

CARL: He's hoping you'll say yes so he can watch.

PAULETTE: Shut up Carl …

JUSTIN: Lesbo alert, lesbo alert!

PAULETTE: Don't get too excited Justin, your diaper might fall off.

RICK: She's not a lesbo, Justin, believe me.

JUSTIN: You never know who she might be fantasizing about when she's kissing you.

TARA: Hey, don't you think if anyone would be able to tell if Paulette was a dyke, it would be me?

JUSTIN: How?

TARA: Think about it.

RICK: 'Cause you'd always be looking at her boobs!

JUSTIN: And you'd weigh about two hundred pounds …

CARL: You'd be bald, pierced, and tattooed everywhere.

PAULETTE: Not all lesbians look like pro wrestlers with boobs. What about k.d. lang?

RICK: She isn't exactly good-looking …

PAULETTE: Yes she is, and she's a great singer too.

JUSTIN: Her music sucks.

TARA: My parents don't want me to buy her CDs.

PAULETTE: Why? Are they afraid if you do you'll turn into a lesbian or something?

TARA: Listen, my mother can't even hear the word homosexual without crossing herself.

RICK: Hey, if me or any of my brothers ever told our parents we were gay, we'd be booted out on our ass before we knew what hit us.

PAULETTE: You think they'd really do that?

RICK: You should have heard my dad last summer when he saw that Gay Pride Day parade on the news. Man, he hit the roof.

CARL: Why do they have to have a friggin' Pride Day in the first place is what I want to know.

JUSTIN: Yeah, what do they have to proud of?

TARA: My mother would have a heart attack if I told her I was a dyke.

PAULETTE: Tara ...

TARA: I bet she'd immediately call a priest to perform an emergency exorcism.

PAULETTE: Why should it make any difference to her if you were gay?

TARA: Get real—my mother? She believes that people like that live in a state of sin because it's against the will of God.

RICK: It says that in the Bible somewhere, doesn't it?

CARL: Who knows? It's not the kind of thing we ever talk about around our house.

TARA: All I know is if the Pope says it's wrong that's good enough for my mom.

PAULETTE: Doesn't she think it's a little weird that the Pope's a single guy who wears a dress all the time?

TARA: No, he's the Pope, that's what popes wear.

PAULETTE: I suppose none of your parents know anybody who's gay?

CARL: My parents? / Yeah, right.

JUSTIN: *(Overlapping.)* No way.

RICK: What about yours?

PAULETTE: Of course. My uncle Greg.

RICK: The guy you introduced me to at your house last week?

PAULETTE: Yes.

RICK: I thought you said he was a cop.

PAULETTE: He is.

CARL: You serious?

PAULETTE: Yes.

JUSTIN: A fag cop?

TARA: Is that legal?

PAULETTE: Of course it is.

RICK: But he didn't act like one.

PAULETTE: What did you expect? He was off duty.

RICK: No, I mean he didn't act like a fag.

PAULETTE: Could you stop saying "fag"? He's my uncle, okay?

RICK: Okay.

CARL: Whose brother is he?

PAULETTE: My dad's.

JUSTIN: And it's cool with him?

PAULETTE: Yeah, and my mom too.

RICK: I've never had a girlfriend who had a gay uncle before.

PAULETTE: And you won't have one for much longer if your attitude doesn't change.

　　(Pause.)

TARA: So is anybody going to buy one of the band's T-shirts?

JUSTIN: With what money?

RICK: Your uncle doesn't care if he gets AIDS?

PAULETTE: I'm sure he thinks about it just as much as anybody else.

TARA: Come, on guys, I don't want to miss the opening act.

RICK: All I'm saying is he's a fa—gay, he could get AIDS …

PAULETTE: Yes—just like anybody else if they don't practice safe sex.

RICK: Yeah, but they kind of started it, right?

　　(PAULETTE walks away.)

　Hey …

PAULETTE: Get away from me …

　　(She exits.)

TARA: You are such an idiot. Paulette, wait up.

　　(TARA exits after her.)

CARL: Way to go man, you really pissed her off.

RICK: She didn't even mention that he was a fag. What did she expect? I mean it's weird, isn't it? Don't you think it's weird?

JUSTIN: I guess fags gotta have relatives too.

CARL: You better tell her you're sorry or she'll be miserable all night.

JUSTIN: Yeah, and I'm planning to make the move on Tara tonight, but there's going to be no way if you guys are fighting.

RICK: Don't waste your time. She hasn't gotten over Carl yet.

JUSTIN: So she can fantasize about him while we're making out, it doesn't matter to me.

RICK: You're an animal.

JUSTIN: Grrrr!

CARL: So you going to tell her you're sorry?

RICK: Yeah, yeah ...

JUSTIN: Then let's go.

(They run off. Concert transition music is heard.)

Scene Three

(We hear the sounds of a crowded hallway. The school bell rings as PAULETTE and TARA enter.)

PAULETTE: Tara, hurry up.

TARA: What's the rush?

PAULETTE: I just want to get to my next class.

TARA: You're trying to avoid Rick, aren't you? Have you talked to him since last night?

PAULETTE: No, and I don't intend to.

TARA: Ever?

PAULETTE: If he doesn't smarten up.

TARA: But he's one of the cutest guys in school.

PAULETTE: Tara, there are more important things in life than just going out with cute guys.

(CARL enters and walks over to them.)

TARA: I know, but they're not as much fun.

CARL: Paulette ...

TARA: Hi Carl.

CARL: Hi. Uh, Rick told me if I saw you to tell you to wait for him at your locker at lunch.

PAULETTE: Well let's pretend you didn't see me, okay?

CARL: You still mad at him?

PAULETTE: I was, but now I'm working on total indifference.

CARL: Didn't he apologize for what he said last night?

PAULETTE: So what? He's still homophobic.

CARL: So what's that got to do with you and him?

PAULETTE: Do you even know what that means?

CARL: Yeah, sure ... it means he doesn't like homos.

PAULETTE: It means he's sexist, and I don't find that very attractive.

TARA: Give the guy a break, Paulette. He's not a total sexist pig just because he doesn't like gays.

PAULETTE: Look, this might be hard for you to understand, but I really care about my uncle. And I know he's been hurt by a lot of ignorant people, who just hate him because he's gay. That's why I can't stand to be around anybody who talks about other people as if they've got no right to live just because they're different. It shouldn't matter if a person's gay—straight—tall—short—cross-eyed—three-headed—buck-toothed—or part amphibian. People are people and they deserve to be treated with respect.

CARL: Jeez, lighten up. It's not like he really believes they don't have a right to live.

PAULETTE: You ever ask him?

CARL: Now you're being stupid.

PAULETTE: Am I? He didn't care how those guys felt being called fags last night. Neither did you.

TARA: Okay, Paulette, you made your point. I think Carl understands how you feel. Now can we maybe talk about something else like ... Are you going to come over to my place and watch videos Saturday night?

CARL: Ummm ...

TARA: Everybody else is coming. Paulette's coming, aren't you Paulette?

PAULETTE: I haven't decided yet.

(RICK and JUSTIN enter.)

RICK: There you are. I've been looking for you all morning.

PAULETTE: I've got to get to my next class.

RICK: Are we meeting at lunch?

PAULETTE: I can't ...

RICK: Why not?

JUSTIN: We're going to my place to make grilled cheese sandwiches. You wanna come Tara?

TARA: Ahhh ...

PAULETTE: Sorry, I gotta go. *(She moves to exit.)* You coming Tara?

TARA: Ah, yeah ... Sorry, maybe next time.

(The girls exit.)

CARL: She's still mad at you.

RICK: Yeah, I figured that out, but how many times am I supposed to say I'm sorry her uncle's gay?

JUSTIN: Is that what you told her?

RICK: Don't be stupid. I tried to tell her I was sorry but ...

CARL: She didn't believe you.

RICK: So what am I supposed to do? Say I love fags or something?

JUSTIN: Maybe she really is a lesbian.

RICK: Will you shut up?

CARL: What are you going to do?

RICK: I don't know.

CARL: Ummm, well why don't you try calling her at home tonight and uh ... tell her that ... you know she cares about her uncle ...

RICK: Yeah ...

CARL: And ummm ... You've thought about what you said and you realized that you were being insensitive.

RICK: Oh that's good.

CARL: Say that it's cool for him to live the kind of life he chooses ... and even though you don't understand it ...

JUSTIN: Are you really going to say that?

RICK: Shut up.

CARL: Oh yeah, and that you really don't hate anybody just because they're different ... and you've got to say it like you mean it, right?

RICK: Think it'll work?

CARL: Depends on how much you want it to.

JUSTIN: Yeah, but we know what he really wants.

RICK: And that's probably something that you won't experience until you finally save enough money to pay for it.

CARL: Look, I've got to get to my next class ...

RICK: Yeah, me too.

CARL: Catch you guys at lunch?

JUSTIN: Yeah.

RICK: Thanks Carl.

CARL: No problem. See you later.

> *(The bell rings as they all exit. The sound of the bell transforms into the sound of a doorbell.)*

Scene Four

(Tara's house, Saturday night. TARA and JUSTIN enter.)

TARA: You're early.

JUSTIN: Am I?

TARA: We said nine.

JUSTIN: Oh ... So nobody else is here?

TARA: Not yet.

JUSTIN: Guess we'll have to find something to do until the others get here, huh?

TARA: What do you have in mind?

JUSTIN: Your parents home?

TARA: No, they went out for the night.

JUSTIN: Then maybe we could just ...

(He moves toward her.)

TARA: What are you doing?

JUSTIN: I was going to ... you know ...

TARA: What?

JUSTIN: Uh ...

TARA: Were you going to kiss me?

JUSTIN: Uh ... yeah ... I guess so ...

TARA: Justin, I like you and everything, but not in that way.

JUSTIN: Oh, sure, I understand ...

TARA: I'm still kind of interested in someone else.

JUSTIN: Yeah, sure ... Sorry ... *(Beat.)* Oh, by the way, Carl's not coming over tonight.

TARA: How do you know?

JUSTIN: I talked to him on the phone today.

TARA: Oh, you talked to him earlier ...

JUSTIN: Yeah ...

TARA: And when you were talking to him did you happen to tell him you thought things might turn out better for you if he didn't show up tonight?

JUSTIN: What are you talking about?

TARA: Forget it, just forget it.

JUSTIN: Look, don't get mad at me because he had something else to do.

TARA: I couldn't care less about what Carl's doing tonight.

JUSTIN: Okay, if you say so.

TARA: I'm going to make some popcorn.

JUSTIN: Want me to help?

TARA: No.

>   *(The doorbell rings.)*

>   Will you get it?

JUSTIN: Sure.

>   *(JUSTIN exits. We hear the voices of the others.)*

RICK: *(Offstage.)* Hey, Justin, what's going on? You head of the house now?

JUSTIN: *(Offstage.)* Yeah, right.

>   *(TARA exits.)*

PAULETTE: *(Offstage.)* Where's Tara?

>   *(They enter.)*

JUSTIN: Making popcorn. What movies did you get?

RICK: I was going to get *Night of the Slasher* …

JUSTIN: Seen it …

RICK: But instead I nabbed a new one just released on video, *Dream Crawler Three: Disemboweler in the City.*

PAULETTE: The plot sounds incredibly stupid so let's watch the one I picked first.

RICK: I don't care which one you put on first because we won't be watching much of either one will we?

>   *(RICK puts his arms around PAULETTE as TARA enters.)*

TARA: Oh great. Are you two going to start making out before we even start the video?

PAULETTE: Hi Tara.

TARA: Hi.

RICK: Why don't we throw on *Dream Crawler* now and save … what's it called?

PAULETTE: *Night Zoo* …

RICK: For when Carl gets here.

JUSTIN: He's not coming.

RICK: Why not?

JUSTIN: He said he had to do some family thing, I don't know.

RICK: Boring. But we can still have fun without him, can't we?

(RICK pulls PAULETTE to him.)

PAULETTE: Hey ...

RICK: Can't we? Hmmm?

PAULETTE: Maybe, if you're a good boy.

RICK: Oh, I'll be good. *(He kisses her.)*

TARA: Guys, are we going to have to watch you suck face all night?

RICK: You don't have to watch us. What do you think the videos are for?

PAULETTE: Rick ...

RICK: What?

PAULETTE: Just cool your jets for a bit.

RICK: Okay, but just because Carl didn't show up doesn't mean she has to take it out on us.

TARA: You didn't tell him, did you?

RICK: It's not like I couldn't figure it out myself.

TARA: I asked you specifically not to tell Rick.

RICK: She just asked me if Carl ever talked about you.

TARA: And you told Carl?

RICK: Forget about Carl. What about Justin?

TARA: What about him?

JUSTIN: Leave me out of it. Why don't we start the video?

RICK: Whatever ...

TARA: You planned this, didn't you?

JUSTIN: Planned what?

TARA: You asked Carl not to come figuring since he wasn't here I'd make out with you, right?

JUSTIN: No ...

TARA: Then why were you early?

JUSTIN: I just got here first.

RICK: Will you get real? Justin's not smart enough to plan something that complicated.

JUSTIN: You saying I'm stupid?

TARA: I don't think I'm in the mood to do this any more.

PAULETTE: Oh come on, Tara, I'm sure they didn't plan this.

TARA: How do you know?

RICK: Jeez, get a grip. You're starting to sound paranoid.

TARA: I think you're going to have to find somewhere else to have your smooch fest.

JUSTIN: We didn't plan this, I swear.

TARA: I don't care.

    (She exits.)

JUSTIN: Rick, tell her we didn't plan this—We didn't plan this, did we?

PAULETTE: I think you guys better leave.

RICK: What about you?

PAULETTE: I'm going to stay with Tara.

RICK: Why?

JUSTIN: We really didn't plan this, Paulette, I swear …

PAULETTE: Because she's upset.

RICK: She'll get over it.

JUSTIN: Paulette—

PAULETTE: I'm not going to leave her alone.

RICK: But I've got my dad's car—we could drive around or something.

JUSTIN: Just tell her we didn't …

RICK: Will you shut up about that already?

PAULETTE: Why don't you and Justin go for a drive?

RICK: This is not happening, this is not happening.

PAULETTE: Call me in a couple of hours. Maybe by then I'll be able to get her to change her mind.

RICK: What if she doesn't?

PAULETTE: You're just going to have to wait and see.

RICK: Aw, come on …

    (RICK and PAULETTE kiss.)

PAULETTE: I'll be waiting for your call.

RICK: Okay … let's go.

JUSTIN: I didn't even get any popcorn.

    (They exit. Transition music.)

Scene Five

(The transition music becomes ambient street noise. RICK and JUSTIN are cruising downtown.)

RICK: You can't be serious. You're telling me you saw your mother naked?

JUSTIN: Yeah, I walked in on her in the bathroom once when she was drying up after a bath.

RICK: You saw everything?

JUSTIN: Yeah.

RICK: And?

JUSTIN: No way.

RICK: I just want to know what her …

JUSTIN: No.

RICK: Why not?

JUSTIN: Because she's my mother, that's why.

> *(Beat.)*

RICK: Hey, look over there …

> *(RICK points at somebody on the sidewalk.)*

Hey faggot, where's your boyfriend?

JUSTIN: He's talking to you, faggot! Look, he's freaking. *(Pause.)* Hey Rick, look.

RICK: What?

JUSTIN: Over there.

RICK: Holy fu—it can't be …

> *(RICK and JUSTIN stare slack-jawed at someone on the street.)*

JUSTIN: It is.

RICK: He's taking off.

JUSTIN: Follow him.

RICK: I've gotta wait for the car in front of me to move, dummy.

JUSTIN: He's getting away.

RICK: Can you still see him?

JUSTIN: Yeah, but we're going to lose him.

> *(Car horns blare.)*

RICK: Come on, come on, asshole! Is this guy in front of us sleeping? I'm freaked, man.

JUSTIN: Rick, the light's changed.

RICK: What? Oh, right … totally freaked …

JUSTIN: Yeah, me too.

> *(Car horns blast as RICK and JUSTIN exit.)*

Scene Six

(Tara's house. PAULETTE and TARA enter.)

TARA: What could be so important that he couldn't tell you it over the phone?

PAULETTE: I don't know. All he said was that they saw something freaky downtown.

TARA: He's just made something up so they can come over.

PAULETTE: No, he really sounded upset.

TARA: They better not be expecting to have a make-out party.

PAULETTE: We'll just kick them out if they try.

(The doorbell rings.)

TARA: I just know this is going to be so bogus. *(TARA exits.)* I want them in and out of here as fast as possible.

PAULETTE: Will you just open the door and let them in, God.

(We hear TARA talking offstage.)

TARA: *(Offstage.)* Well, look who it is. I thought you couldn't make it?

(TARA and CARL enter.)

CARL: Oh yeah, well I escaped and I thought I'd drop by. How were the videos?

PAULETTE: We didn't watch them.

CARL: So where are the guys?

PAULETTE: They're on their way over.

CARL: They haven't been here yet?

TARA: They were here …

PAULETTE: But we needed a little time by ourselves …

(The doorbell rings.)

TARA: That's them now.

(TARA exits again.)

CARL: Did you and Rick have another fight or something?

PAULETTE: Ah no, not really … Tara and I just needed to talk … you know, personal stuff.

(We hear the voices of the others.)

RICK: *(Offstage.)* Man, this is so mind-blowing. Where's Paulette?

TARA: *(Offstage.)* In the living room.

JUSTIN: *(Offstage.)* I would never have believed it unless I saw it myself.

(They enter.)

RICK: Paulette ...

CARL: Hi guys. What's going on? What are you looking at? Did I grow another head or something?

RICK: What are you doing here?

CARL: I thought maybe you'd still be watching videos.

JUSTIN: Didn't you have something better to do?

RICK: Yeah, something with your "family"?

PAULETTE: Why are you guys acting so weird?

RICK: So how's the "family," Carl?

CARL: Fine ...

JUSTIN: What did you do? Go downtown for a big "family" dinner?

CARL: No, we ate at home.

RICK: You sure.

CARL: Why wouldn't I be?

RICK: We thought maybe you and the "family" went downtown for a little walk on the wild side.

TARA: Will you tell us what you're talking about?

RICK: Carl knows what I'm talking about, don't you?

CARL: No, as a matter of fact, I don't.

RICK: Then let me fill you in. You see, when Justin and I left here earlier we thought we'd drive downtown to kill some time and we happened to drive up Church Street ... You know what's on Church Street, don't you?

JUSTIN: Don't bother trying to pretend you don't know what kind of bars are on that street ...

RICK: Because who do you think we saw hanging out there with all the other fags? *(Beat.)* Come on, guess.

(CARL moves to exit and RICK steps in his way.)

Didn't you hear us calling you?

JUSTIN: We tried to get your attention when we saw you leaving the steps of the Second Cup.

TARA: Oh come on, this is one of your sick jokes.

RICK: Is it, Carl? Or are you a fag who goes to Church Street to pick up other fags? Is that why you were there?

CARL: Shut up, Rick ...

RICK: You going to make me, queerboy?

PAULETTE: Rick, leave him alone. Just because he was on Church Street doesn't mean—

RICK: Oh, we didn't just see him on the street ...

JUSTIN: We followed him and saw him go in some fag bar called The Barn.

TARA: How do you know what kind of bar it was?

RICK: Because we saw other fags going in with him.

PAULETTE: Maybe you made a mistake. It could have been someone else.

TARA: Why don't you say something?

RICK: Because it was you, wasn't it?

CARL: Get out of my way.

RICK: Make me.

TARA: Come on, guys. I don't want you to wreck the place, my parents are going to be home any second ...

JUSTIN: Don't make him bleed, Rick, you could get AIDS.

PAULETTE: This is gross, stop it!

RICK: You want to fight me, faggot?

CARL: I just want to get out of here.

PAULETTE: Let him go, Rick ...

> *(TARA grabs a portable phone.)*

TARA: I swear if you start fighting in here I'll call the cops. Guys, I'm dialing. Hello?

RICK: Okay, okay ...

> *(RICK moves out of CARL's way. CARL leaves quickly.)*

You better run, faggot!

PAULETTE: Shut up, Rick. God, he's your friend.

RICK: Are you nuts? I don't have faggots for friends.

PAULETTE: What about all those things you said to me on the phone?

RICK: We were talking about your uncle. Not one of my ex-best friends who I trusted ... who I thought I knew ...

PAULETTE: He's still the same person.

RICK: Except he's a fag, and that's supposed to be cool, right? Sorry, it's not.

PAULETTE: You better leave—and don't bother calling me again.

RICK: You serious?

> *(PAULETTE exits.)*

TARA: Take a hint, Brainiac, I think she means it.

RICK: Yeah, well I was stupid to call her in the first place. *(RICK moves to exit.)* Maybe you should introduce Carl to your uncle. Wouldn't they make a nice couple?

TARA: Okay, that's enough, Rick, just leave.

RICK: Don't worry, I'm going.

> *(He exits.)*

TARA: You too, Justin.

JUSTIN: What did I do?

RICK: *(Offstage.)* Justin, you want a lift home or you planning to walk?

JUSTIN: Okay, okay, I'm coming.

> *(JUSTIN exits. TARA stands alone on stage. A school bell rings.)*

Scene Seven

> *(A school bell rings and we hear the sounds of students in a crowded hallway.)*

FIRST FEMALE STUDENT: *(Voice-over.)* He's gay? Get out of here, I don't / believe it.

SECOND FEMALE STUDENT: *(Voice-over, overlapping.)* Who told you?

FIRST MALE STUDENT: *(Voice-over.)* They said they saw him walk right out / of the place.

FIRST FEMALE STUDENT: *(Voice-over, overlapping.)* I necked with him once at a party. I never would have guessed in a million years / that he was …

FIRST MALE STUDENT: *(Voice-over, overlapping.)* If it's true then we were all taking showers after gym with a fag.

TARA: No I never went out with him—I thought he was cute, so what? We were just / friends.

> *(RICK enters.)*

RICK: *(Overlapping.)* Friends? Are you nuts? Yeah, I said it right to her face. I mean, what did she expect, the guy's a / freak.

(JUSTIN enters.)

JUSTIN: *(Overlapping.)* Freaked us out when we first spotted him. I'm surprised he showed up at school today. I mean, he must have known Rick was going to tell / everybody.

(PAULETTE enters.)

PAULETTE: *(Overlapping.)* Everybody is talking about it so why should you be any different? Yes, I broke up with Rick. No, he didn't dump me. I don't know if it's true, I wasn't in the car when they say they saw him.

TARA: I was not—will you get real—hot for him? Okay, I might have said I liked him but that was because he pretended he was interested in me. Yeah, I guess I do feel kind of used.

(CARL enters and they all stop talking. Pause. They all stare at him.)

CARL: Oh, don't stop on my account. It's not like I don't know what you were talking about.

FIRST FEMALE STUDENT: *(Voice-over.)* So is it true?

CARL: I can't believe you're asking me this.

(PAULETTE exits.)

FIRST MALE STUDENT: *(Voice-over.)* Why would Rick and Justin lie about something like that?

CARL: Who knows? Rick's always getting pissed off about something.

(TARA exits.)

SECOND FEMALE STUDENT: *(Voice-over.)* So it wasn't you they saw?

CARL: I told you ...

(JUSTIN exits.)

FIRST MALE STUDENT: *(Voice-over.)* Did you hear about the fight?

(RICK exits.)

SECOND MALE STUDENT: *(Voice-over.)* I hope Rick kicks the crap out of him, because if he doesn't, I will.

FIRST FEMALE STUDENT: *(Voice-over.)* Think he'll show up for the fight?

SECOND FEMALE STUDENT: *(Voice-over.)* If he doesn't we'll just go and find him.

FIRST MALE STUDENT: *(Voice-over.)* Faggot.

SECOND FEMALE STUDENT: *(Voice-over.)* Homo.

SECOND MALE STUDENT: *(Voice-over.)* Fairy.

FIRST FEMALE STUDENT: *(Voice-over.)* Queer.

ALL: *(Together.)* Fag, homo, fairy, queer! Fag, homo, fairy, queer! *Fag, homo, fairy, queer! Fag, homo, fairy, queer!! Fight!! Fight!! Fight!!*

> *(The chanting reaches a crescendo and ends abruptly at the sound of a slamming door. We hear the voice-overs of MARION and FRANK.)*

MARION: Carl, is that you?

CARL: Yeah, sorry I'm late.

> *(He moves to exit.)*

MARION: Carl ...

CARL: Yeah?

MARION: We got some disturbing phone calls today ...

CARL: From who?

MARION: Some kids. I thought I recognized some of their voices ... I wasn't sure ...

CARL: What were they calling about?

MARION: Are you in some kind of trouble with a gang at school?

CARL: No.

MARION: Then why were those boys calling here?

CARL: I don't know.

MARION: I didn't say anything to your father because I wanted to talk to you about it first.

CARL: I don't know why they were calling.

MARION: They kept asking if ... they were saying things about you ...

CARL: I just got into a fight with one of the guys at school, that's all ...

MARION: Why were you fighting?

CARL: Mom, can we talk about this later? Please?

MARION: Okay, go and get cleaned up.

> *(CARL moves to exit as the phone rings. He stops. We hear Carl's father answering the phone. CARL listens.)*

FRANK: Hello? What? Who is this? Hello? Hello?

> *(We hear a dial tone.)*

Where's Carl?

MARION: Washing up.

FRANK: Some kid just called.

MARION: They've been calling all day.

FRANK: All day?

MARION: He was in a fight and now some kids are trying to get back at him.

FRANK: Little creeps.

MARION: That's all he would tell me.

FRANK: You think it's serious?

MARION: I don't know.

CARL: And then we all sit down to dinner and nobody says anything until the phone starts ringing again and Dad gets up to answer it. I can see he's ready to explode but he doesn't. He's listening to the person talking but he doesn't say anything. Instead he puts the receiver down and waits by the phone for a few seconds—picks it up, dials "star 69," and the phone automatically re-connects with the person who last called our number. He starts talking—now yelling at some kid's father—Mom and I just sit and listen until he slams the phone down in disgust and comes back to the table. Feels like the oxygen has left the room. He's sitting right there looking at me but he seems a million miles away—almost as if he's checking to see if there's anything different about me from a long distance. Can't let him see how scared I am so I start eating even though the food's sticking in my throat like wallpaper paste. "Dad, you going to eat those potatoes or can I have them? Your potatoes—you going to eat them? Hey, I'm sorry about the phone calls. Um, you know how it is. I got in a fight after a basketball game 'cause the other guys sucked and now they're spreading this stupid lie or rumour or whatever." He's back, like he snapped out of a spell—"Look, I'll straighten it out tomorrow at school, okay? So don't let it bum you out and ruin your dinner 'cause it's not worth thinking about ... Hey, if you don't think you can eat that other pork chop I've got plenty of room." Suddenly we're back to normal again. He's telling us about some rumour somebody spread about him in university. My mother's laughing because she remembers. By the end of dinner I have two helpings of everything and we're all in a good mood. Then I tell them I'm going upstairs to study but instead I go into the washroom and throw everything up until I think I'm going to start heaving internal organs because I have no idea how long it's going to be before they find out who was really lying.

(The sound of phones ringing is heard. After a few beats the sound of phones transforms into the sound of a school bell ringing.)

Scene Eight

(School hallway. CARL moves to exit as PAULETTE calls him from off stage.)

PAULETTE: Carl. *(Entering.)* Hey, wait up.

CARL: What do you want?

PAULETTE: How about a simple "hello" for starters?

CARL: Hi.

(He moves to exit.)

PAULETTE: Where are you going?

CARL: Home.

PAULETTE: Mind if I walk with you?

CARL: Sure you want to be seen with me?

PAULETTE: Why wouldn't I?

CARL: I'm not one of the most popular people here lately.

PAULETTE: Neither am I since I broke up with Rick.

CARL: You guys really broke up?

PAULETTE: Please, he's such a jerk.

CARL: Yeah, so who isn't, right?

PAULETTE: How can you say that after the way he's been treating you? Last week you guys were best friends—everybody liked you—and now they're treating you like …

CARL: Steve … Bosco?

PAULETTE: Steve who?

CARL: Bosco. He went to school here a couple of years ago and got labelled a fag because he popped a boner in the showers. I was there when it happened. I was getting dressed after gym and I heard the other guys yelling, "Check out the faggot with the boner!" Everybody was chasing him around—whacking him with wet towels—and he was dying from embarrassment. It's not like he tried to come on to anybody or anything. I'm sure it was like a total accident but nobody ever let him live it down.

PAULETTE: Did you talk to him about it?

CARL: Yeah, right. Once he was labelled a fag nobody talked to him and I watched how people treated him.

PAULETTE: How did you treat him?

CARL: I called him "Bum-boy Bosco" like everyone else. What are you looking at me like that for? I know it sucks, but what else was I supposed to do?

PAULETTE: I don't know, I wasn't there.

CARL: You probably would've said something to defend him, knowing you. You've got the guts to say what you think.

PAULETTE: So what happened to this Steve Bosco guy?

CARL: I think his family moved or something because he didn't come back the following year. Man it really freaked me when all that was going on, too, because that was just around the time ... What the hell am I doing? Why am I telling you this?

PAULETTE: What's wrong?

CARL: Look, what are you trying to prove? That you're cool enough to have a fag friend or something?

PAULETTE: Isn't just wanting to be your friend enough?

(Pause.)

CARL: Guess I can't afford to be picky, can I?

PAULETTE: Thanks a lot.

CARL: I didn't mean it that way ...

PAULETTE: Look, you don't have to tell me if you don't want to.

CARL: No ... I want to ... So anyway around the time that all that crap was happening to that Bosco guy I was just beginning to realize that I was having the kinds of thoughts—feelings that everybody says you're not supposed to have, you know ...

PAULETTE: About sex?

CARL: Yeah ... and I couldn't help it. I knew I was supposed to be having these thoughts about girls but I wasn't.

PAULETTE: Did it scare you?

CARL: The thoughts didn't, but the idea of anyone finding out I was having them did. So I tried to stop myself from having them. I tried praying as hard as I could for them to go away but they just kept getting stronger and stronger. At night I'd lie awake in bed and try to pull all those thoughts and feelings together in my mind and shoot them out of me like a laser beam into outer space.

PAULETTE: And what happened when you did that?

CARL: I got a headache.

PAULETTE: So have you ever had a boyfriend or anything?

CARL: Shut up.

PAULETTE: What's wrong?

CARL: I've had girlfriends, you know.

PAULETTE: So? That doesn't mean you couldn't have boyfriends too.

CARL: Will you shut up?

PAULETTE: Why are you so embarrassed?

CARL: Because ...

PAULETTE: So you've never even kissed a guy or anything?

CARL: Paulette ...

PAULETTE: Well?

CARL: You're too much, you know that? *(Beat.)* Okay, I've had a few experiences, but it was just kid stuff.

PAULETTE: You've never talked to anybody about this, have you?

CARL: I've called a Gay Youth Line a couple of times.

PAULETTE: Is that like a hot line or something?

CARL: I found out about it in *Extra,* a free gay magazine you can get just about anywhere downtown ... I snuck a copy home one day.

PAULETTE: And what about when the guys saw you that night?

CARL: What about it? I wanted to see what that kind of place was like ... I ... Okay, I'd been there once before.

PAULETTE: At that bar?

CARL: Yeah, Saturday was my second time.

PAULETTE: So what's it like?

CARL: Just like any other bar, I guess, except there were only two women in it that I could see. You know I don't hate women?

PAULETTE: Duh.

CARL: I know that's what some people think ... Anyway I didn't really think I'd get in the first time I went but the guy at the door didn't even bother asking for my ID. Then suddenly I'm in the place and my heart's in my mouth because I don't know what to expect. I mean for all I knew I could've been walking into an orgy palace. So I'm ready to run out at the first sign of weirdness. But then I'm looking around at all these different types of guys having a good time just like anybody. Like it's no big deal or anything. I didn't stay long though. I was too nervous. It was enough just to walk in the door. That was about two months ago. I tried to forget about it.

PAULETTE: But you couldn't.

CARL: No ... *(Beat.)* So I went back and ... you know the rest.

PAULETTE: Are you going there Friday night?

CARL: I don't think I'll be going back for quite a while.

PAULETTE: Then are you going to go to the school dance?

CARL: Hey, I'm gay, not stupid.

PAULETTE: I'd like to go ... but I don't have a date.

CARL: You saying that because you want me to go with you?

PAULETTE: Would you?

CARL: Are you nuts?

PAULETTE: Why not? Come on, you're brave enough to go to a gay bar, but not the dance?

CARL: It's not the same and you know it.

PAULETTE: Carl, you've got just as much right to be there as anybody else.

CARL: I used to think I did.

PAULETTE: Unless you show people that you've got no reason to be ashamed they're going to treat you exactly the way they treated that Steve Bosco guy. All you have to do is show up.

CARL: I'll think about it.

(They exit.)

Scene Nine

(The dance. Dance music plays. JUSTIN enters, tugging TARA by the arm. The music fades into the background and continues to play throughout the scene.)

JUSTIN: No, no way. I hate dancing to that crap.

TARA: Aw, you said you'd dance with me tonight ...

JUSTIN: I will, but not to that.

TARA: So what do you want to do then?

JUSTIN: I'm sure we can find something interesting to do while we wait for something better to dance to ...

(He puts his arms around her.)

TARA: Like what?

JUSTIN: Like this ...

(He moves to kiss her as RICK enters.)

RICK: Come on, you two, break it up.

JUSTIN: Hi Rick ...

RICK: Sorry, didn't mean to interrupt your lip lock.

TARA: Then why did you?

RICK: Because I need to talk to your new boyfriend.

JUSTIN: What about?

RICK: Beer.

JUSTIN: Cool.

RICK: Want to help me polish off a six-pack?

TARA: Where'd you get it?

JUSTIN: His brother probably got it for him. Didn't he?

RICK: He owed me a favour. Come on, let's go before they get warm.

JUSTIN: You coming?

TARA: No, I hate beer, but you go if you want to.

JUSTIN: You sure?

TARA: I told Paulette I'd meet her here, so I'll just hang out and wait for her.

RICK: You still hanging out with that loser?

TARA: She's my friend. And it's none of your business who I hang out with anyway.

RICK: What kind of friend?

TARA: You're twisted.

(RICK starts to exit.)

RICK: Oh, don't be mad at me, les—be—friends.

TARA: Why be friends? I'm sure you'd rather be at homo alone, playing with yourself.

JUSTIN: Good comeback.

RICK: Ha ha ... *(He exits.)* You coming for a beer or what?

JUSTIN: I'll just have one and I'll be right back.

TARA: They won't let you back in if they smell beer on your breath.

(TARA gives him some gum.)

JUSTIN: Thanks.

TARA: I hope he's not going to be putting Paulette down all night.

JUSTIN: I'll ask him to quit it, okay?

(PAULETTE enters.)

TARA: Don't be long.

JUSTIN: I won't.

(He exits.)

PAULETTE: Hi …

TARA: You look great.

PAULETTE: Thanks, so do you. So how's it going?

TARA: All these dances are the same.

PAULETTE: No, I mean you and Justin.

TARA: Isn't it funny? He was hanging around the whole time I was moping over Carl and I didn't pay any attention to him.

PAULETTE: And now?

TARA: So far we're having fun.

PAULETTE: He is kind of cute.

TARA: Think so?

PAULETTE: Oh yeah.

TARA: He's a good kisser too.

PAULETTE: Really?

TARA: Would I lie to you about something like that, girlfriend?

PAULETTE: Who'd have thought?

TARA: Not me, girl.

PAULETTE: So where'd he go?

TARA: Rick brought some beer.

PAULETTE: Same old Rick.

TARA: I'm glad you decided to come.

PAULETTE: Me too, but I hope I don't get stood up.

TARA: You have a date? Who?

PAULETTE: You'll see.

TARA: Come on, tell me who it is. Is it Gord? Dean? I know, it's Robert Morgan.

PAULETTE: Nope.

TARA: Then who?

(CARL enters.)

PAULETTE: Here he is now.

TARA: Carl? Paulette, are you nuts? What's everybody going to think?

PAULETTE: I don't know and I don't care either.

CARL: Hi ... How you doing, Tara?

TARA: Okay ...

PAULETTE: How's it going?

CARL: I'm still not sure this was such a good idea. You should have seen the stares I got when I walked in.

PAULETTE: We'll really give them something to stare at when we're dancing.

CARL: I don't know ...

PAULETTE: We've got to dance. That's what we came here for.

CARL: We'll see.

> *(JUSTIN enters. He hesitates before he approaches them and after a beat walks over.)*

TARA: I was beginning to think you'd forgotten about me.

JUSTIN: No chance of that.

> *(Pause.)*

PAULETTE: Aren't you guys going to say hi to each other? *(Pause.)* Justin?

JUSTIN: Uh, hi.

CARL: Hi.

PAULETTE: Carl, let's go and dance.

CARL: Uh ...

> *(She pulls him along.)*

PAULETTE: We'll see you in there.

> *(They exit.)*

JUSTIN: What's he doing here?

TARA: I'm sure it was Paulette's idea.

JUSTIN: It's like they're both just asking for trouble.

TARA: Well you know it'd be useless trying to talk them into leaving. Once she makes her mind up about something nobody can change it. So let's just mind our own business and dance.

> *(She tries to tug him toward the gym but he doesn't budge.)*

JUSTIN: I told Rick we'd wait here for him.

TARA: I thought I was your date.

JUSTIN: What's that supposed to mean?

TARA: Can't you do anything without Rick?

JUSTIN: Look, I don't want to argue. We'll duck out in a bit. Just you and me, okay?

(*RICK enters.*)

RICK: Hey, did I see what I thought I saw in the gym?

JUSTIN: Yeah, we saw him too.

RICK: Doesn't he know fags aren't welcome here?

JUSTIN: What's the big deal? He's not bothering anyone.

RICK: Are you going soft on queers now or something?

JUSTIN: No, but can't we just forget about it tonight and have a good time?

RICK: Good idea. Tara, you wanna dance?

TARA: What are you up to, Rick?

RICK: Here I am trying to have a good time like Justin suggested and you're, like, so suspicious. I guess I'll just have to go in and dance by myself.

(*RICK exits.*)

TARA: What's he going to do?

JUSTIN: I don't know.

(*The music grows in volume and we hear the sounds of screams, yells, and catcalls in the mix. We hear voices chanting, "Fight, fight, fight," etc. JUSTIN and TARA run off. The music fades until all we hear are the voices chanting.*)

Scene Ten

(*Carl's house. The chanting and catcalls reach a crescendo as the sound of a roaring car motor enters the mix. CARL runs onstage and stops. We hear a door slam and the motor stops. We hear the voice-overs of MARION and FRANK.*)

MARION: Is he all right?

FRANK: He's fine.

MARION: What happened?

FRANK: He was fighting with Rick Bowman at the dance.

MARION: Rick? But ...

FRANK: His principal said he's been having trouble getting along with the other students lately.

MARION: Does he know why?

FRANK: Those phone calls we were getting ...

MARION: What about them?

FRANK: Rick seemed to know why those kids were saying those things ...

MARION: About Carl?

FRANK: I'm going to bed.

MARION: But ...

FRANK: We'll talk about it tomorrow.

MARION: He needs us now.

FRANK: God damn it, Marion, we'll talk about it tomorrow.

(We hear the sound of a door slamming. CARL steps forward.)

MARION: I thought you went up to your room?

CARL: Just about to.

(He moves to exit.)

MARION: I want you to talk to me.

CARL: What about?

MARION: What's been happening at school—with your friends—

CARL: I don't—

MARION: You and Rick were fighting. Your father said it had something to do with those phone calls we were getting.

CARL: What if it did? Eh? What if that's exactly what it was about? Mom, I don't ... it's ... Mom, I'm gay.

MARION: You're ...? How do you know?

CARL: Mom, I know, okay?

MARION: But how can you be sure? Have you ... I mean are you ... oh my God, oh my God ...

CARL: Mom ...

MARION: Are you having safe sex?

CARL: Mom ...

MARION: Answer me ...

CARL: If I was having sex ... with anybody, it would be safe ...

MARION: Don't lie to me.

CARL: I'm not lying ...

(She begins to cry.)

Don't cry ... please don't cry ...

MARION: I'm sorry, it's just ... I didn't know ...

CARL: Mom ...

MARION: The thought of you getting that disease—of not knowing this about my own child ...

CARL: I'm sorry Mom, I'm really sorry ...

MARION: No, no, no you don't have to be sorry ... How did they find out? Did you tell them?

CARL: No. It doesn't matter how they found out. They just did. And I don't think I can go back.

MARION: What do you mean?

CARL: To school—I can't take it any more.

MARION: Now hold on just a minute—

CARL: You don't understand! I can't walk down the hall without being called something—You don't have a clue what it's like—I mean I can't fight everybody—believe me, I've tried.

MARION: Then I'll go down to that school and talk to the principal.

CARL: And what do you expect him to do?

MARION: We'll find out. Monday we're going to your school and we'll deal with this together.

CARL: What about Dad?

MARION: It'll be okay. I'll talk to him.

(He moves to exit.)

Love you.

CARL: Love you too.

(CARL moves to exit as we hear transition music and the sounds of a busy street.)

Scene Eleven

(On the street. PAULETTE enters and runs to catch up with CARL.)

PAULETTE: Hey ...

CARL: Do me a favour, will you? Just leave me alone.

PAULETTE: I'm sorry about what happened at the dance.

CARL: I should have known better. I'm such an idiot!

PAULETTE: You're not ...

CARL: Look, I don't need your pity, okay?

PAULETTE: I wasn't offering it.

CARL: What is it with you, eh? Why are you always trying to prove what a good person you are?

PAULETTE: I'm not—

CARL: Saint Paulette!

PAULETTE: I was just trying to …

CARL: Yeah, yeah, I know, you were just trying to help.

PAULETTE: I said I was sorry …

CARL: You weren't really trying to help me—you were just trying to prove how superior you are—that's what this is all about for you—

PAULETTE: Okay, I was wrong. Is that what you want to hear? Or that Rick's right and all the fags and dykes should be put on an island somewhere where they wouldn't bother the rest of us normal folks?

CARL: I just want to be left alone.

(He moves to exit.)

PAULETTE: All right, I admit it! I'm a self-centered egotistical bitch who has to prove how superior she is all the time.

CARL: You just don't give up do you?

PAULETTE: I've been worried … you haven't talked to me and I was wondering what was going on …

CARL: What's been going on? Let's see. Monday my mom dragged me to the principal's office—she talked, he nodded and looked concerned—then told her he'd see what he could do about it but the school couldn't be held responsible for what happened off of school property. For some reason I just don't think it was a big priority for him. What else? Oh yeah, my dad hasn't talked to me since the night of the dance.

PAULETTE: Your father's not talking to you?

CARL: Hey, he never had much to say anyway. Except the next morning after the dance when my mother told him about my situation.

(We hear FRANK's voice-over.)

FRANK: Is this something he's going around telling everybody?

CARL: He knew I was in the house but it didn't matter.

FRANK: He's just a kid for Christ's sake! He's probably just confused.

CARL: I've never heard him talk like that before.

FRANK: Is he even willing to try and change? Or has he made up his mind to live like that and we're just supposed to accept it? Well, I'm not sure I can.

CARL: He hasn't said anything to me since.

PAULETTE: Carl …

CARL: I'm sick of feeling like I don't belong anywhere.

PAULETTE: I know it's really hard for you right now but …

CARL: Look, you've never had your father and just about everybody else you thought were your friends turn their backs on you so don't tell me you know how hard it must be for me because you don't. I'm starting to think that maybe I should just do everybody a favour and disappear.

PAULETTE: What are you talking about? *(Beat.)* You're not thinking about taking off are you?

CARL: What if I am?

PAULETTE: Carl, listen to me—listen—I told my Uncle Greg what's been happening …

CARL: Sure, why not? Everybody else knows?

PAULETTE: He told me he has a friend who's involved with this alternative educational program.

CARL: So?

PAULETTE: That's been especially created for gay—

CARL: No.

PAULETTE: Gay and lesbian students—will you at least listen?

CARL: Forget it.

PAULETTE: It's called the Triangle Program—and—it's for students—listen—it's for students who are having trouble in their regular schools.

CARL: Triangle Program?

PAULETTE: Yes. He got the phone number of their office for me.

CARL: You expect me to call them?

PAULETTE: What have you got to lose?

CARL: Good question.

> *(He exits. PAULETTE stands alone on stage as phones begin to ring.)*

Scene Twelve

(A telephone rings. PAULETTE picks up a cell phone as TARA enters, also holding one. The HOT LINE VOLUNTEER is a voice-over.)

TARA: *(Simultaneously with the VOLUNTEER.)* Hello?

VOLUNTEER: Hello, Gay Lesbian Bi Youth Hot Line …

> *(The line is disconnected and we hear the buzz of the dial tone. After a beat the ringing starts again. JUSTIN enters with a cell phone. CARL enters and stops in an isolated area.)*

JUSTIN: Hello?

PAULETTE: *(Overlapping JUSTIN.)* Hello?

VOLUNTEER: *(Overlapping JUSTIN.)* Hello, Gay Lesbian Bi Youth Hot Line …

> *(Once again the line is disconnected.)*

CARL: I've been having these dreams …

VOLUNTEER: Hello, Gay Lesbian Bi Youth Hot Line, this is Jeff speaking …

PAULETTE: Hello?

CARL: I'm with the guys and we're chasing someone …

TARA: Who is this?

CARL: I can see him running up ahead of us. We're yelling at him at the top of our lungs. Run, faggot, run!

PAULETTE: Where are you?

CARL: He trips and we're on him with our fists like jackhammers …

JUSTIN: Look whoever you are you're going to have to speak up because I can't hear you.

CARL: Bones crushing …

PAULETTE: Have you thought about what I said?

CARL: He's trying to call for help but no one's listening …

TARA: Who is this?

CARL: We're mashing him to nothingness—and the whole time I'm hating doing it but I know if I stop … I'll be next …

JUSTIN: Look, I think you've got the wrong number.

> *(JUSTIN exits.)*

VOLUNTEER: Are you still living at home?

CARL: I wake up covered in sweat …

TARA: Oh, it's you …

VOLUNTEER: Have your parents said anything to make you think they don't want you there?

CARL: I just want to jump out of bed and run as far away as I can …

PAULETTE: Are you still there?

VOLUNTEER: You know there are groups for parents ...

CARL: I want to run back in time before this ever happened ...

PAULETTE: So have you changed your mind about the Triangle Program?

CARL: But the future keeps pulling me forward ...

TARA: Look, I can't talk right now ... it's way too late ... call me some other time okay?

    (TARA exits.)

CARL: Dragging me along ... out of control ...

VOLUNTEER: Listen, unless your life at home is intolerable I would advise you to try and stick it out as long as you can.

CARL: And there's a part of me that wants to just let go and see where it takes me ...

VOLUNTEER: Your father might just need a little more time to accept it.

CARL: Secretly hoping that maybe I'll end up somewhere far away where none of this matters ...

PAULETTE: Are you sure? Carl?

    (The dial tone drones on and transforms into street sounds as PAULETTE exits.)

CARL: Where I won't have to pretend I'm someone I'm not. I wouldn't have to lie about a part of myself that I'm trying to understand.

    (ANTONY and RACHEL enter.)

RACHEL: Antony, it's not funny.

ANTONY: Oh girl, you've got to be kidding. She really said that to you?

CARL: Because now I know no matter what happens ... there's no turning back.

RACHEL: Can you believe it?

ANTONY: So what did you say to her?

RACHEL: I told her she could not take back the ring and shove it. There's no way I was going to keep seeing her if she's going to start seeing her old girlfriend again.

    (We hear the sound of a phone ringing.)

ANTONY: Good for you, girl. I'll bet she'll come crawling back to you on her hands and knees.

(We hear the voice-over of PAULETTE.)

PAULETTE: Hello?

RACHEL: And you know what I'll do if that happens?

CARL: It's me ...

ANTONY: Don't go there, Rachel ...

PAULETTE: It's about time.

RACHEL: Why? What do you think I'll do?

PAULETTE: I was wondering when you were going to call me back—
So?

ANTONY: Probably throw your high principles out the window and
take her back.

RACHEL: Thanks a lot.

CARL: It's different, that's for sure.

ANTONY: I can read your mind.

PAULETTE: Is that good or bad?

RACHEL: Antony, you can barely read a book.

CARL: Some of it's good. Like I didn't know there were so many
important people in history who were gay.

RACHEL: So you don't think I should take her back?

PAULETTE: What about the other kids in the class.

ANTONY: Listen Miss Thing, if my boyfriend told me he wanted to
start dating his ex-boyfriend again—I'd be out of there before he
could finish his last sentence—and I wouldn't look back!

RACHEL: Maybe you're right.

CARL: Well, there's only fifteen of us.

ANTONY: Girl, you know I am.

CARL: I don't really get along with any of them.

PAULETTE: Why not?

ANTONY: Can't you see me sash-shaying out of there?
(He struts off followed by RACHEL.)

CARL: Because there's this guy Antony.

RACHEL: Hey girlfriend, you want some fries with that shake?
(She exits.)

CARL: He acts real faggy. *(Beat.)* And after we saw a documentary
how the Nazis persecuted gays in concentration camps the class
had a discussion and I said ...

PAULETTE: What?

    (Beat.)

CARL: That maybe the Nazis would've left gays alone if the more, you know, queeny ones could've acted normal.

PAULETTE: You didn't.

CARL: It just kind of jumped out of my mouth and Antony went ballistic.

    (ANTONY appears.)

ANTONY: And whose standard of normal would they be judged by, Butch? Yours or Adolf's?

CARL: All I'm saying is, if it would make life easier, why not act normal?

ANTONY: I'll leave the acting for people who have something to hide and just be myself thank you very much.

CARL: You just act like a queen because you want attention.

ANTONY: And you act like a homophobe because you're a fascist, sexist, Nazi pig!

    (ANTONY exits.)

CARL: Then I got into a huge fight with the rest of the class because they all agreed with Antony. And then I kind of pushed him.

PAULETTE: Kind of?

CARL: He pissed me off.

PAULETTE: You going to apologize?

CARL: I just pushed him, I didn't punch him in the face.

PAULETTE: Come on, you said you'd give it a try.

CARL: I am but it's weird.

PAULETTE: It's as weird as you make it. Just think of it as an adventure.

CARL: You mean like, "Carl's adventures at Homo High"?

PAULETTE: Remember, you can always quit if you don't like it.

CARL: Enough already. I'll handle it … So you want to meet me after school tomorrow or what?

PAULETTE: I usually try to avoid hanging around with fascist sexist Nazi pigs but maybe this time I can make an exception.

    (We hear the phone hanging up and CARL exits.)

Scene Thirteen

(School hallway. A school bell rings as JUSTIN and PAULETTE enter.)

JUSTIN: Tara's meeting me in a sec. We're heading over to Greasy Nick's, wanna come?

PAULETTE: I can't, I'm meeting Carl. We're supposed to go to a movie. Or maybe we could all do something together?

JUSTIN: Ah ..

PAULETTE: Aren't you even a little curious about how he's doing?

JUSTIN: Um … yeah, sure …

PAULETTE: Then why don't you come and find out?

JUSTIN: I have to wait for Tara.

PAULETTE: Did he ever come on to you or anything?

JUSTIN: Gross.

PAULETTE: Well, did he?

JUSTIN: No.

PAULETTE: So what are you afraid of?

JUSTIN: Not him, that's for sure.

PAULETTE: Then of what people will think?

JUSTIN: I don't care what other people / think.

PAULETTE: *(Overlapping.)* Doesn't look like it when Rick's around.

JUSTIN: Why are you always trying to piss people off?

PAULETTE: I don't know. It's just something that comes naturally I guess.

JUSTIN: Look, I always liked Carl, but how am I supposed to feel comfortable around him when I know he's …

PAULETTE: Into guys? Because if he's gay then he must be attracted to you right? God, men and their egos. Look do you want to have sex with every girl you see?

JUSTIN: Practically.

PAULETTE: Come on—Lucy Divorski?

JUSTIN: Stop, you'll give me nightmares. Okay, not every girl. So?

PAULETTE: Think about it.

(RICK enters. He spots them and hesitates.)

Look, I gotta go.

(PAULETTE exits.)

RICK: What's up?

JUSTIN: Nothing.

RICK: Where's she going?

JUSTIN: Uh ... to meet someone ...

RICK: Who?

    (Beat.)

JUSTIN: Don't know.

RICK: She seeing someone?

JUSTIN: She didn't say.

RICK: Uh huh ...

JUSTIN: You've been going around calling her a scag since / you broke up ...

RICK: *(Overlapping.)* She is, isn't she?

JUSTIN: What do you care who / she's seeing?

    (TARA enters.)

TARA: *(Overlapping.)* Sorry I'm late.

RICK: So she is.

JUSTIN: I told you ...

RICK: You're useless!

    (RICK exits.)

TARA: What's up with him?

JUSTIN: He's obsessed.

TARA: Don't tell—with Paulette—right?

JUSTIN: Yeah ... I didn't tell him she was going to meet Carl.

TARA: He would've probably flipped out if you did—like when my mother heard about it from one of her friends? God, she just wouldn't shut up about it. "Oh, oh that poor boy's parents—Didn't you used to like a boy named Carl? Blah, blah, blah" ... I think it's probably better for everyone that Carl transferred to another school so maybe everything can get back to normal.

JUSTIN: Just forget he ever existed?

TARA: I'm not saying that.

JUSTIN: Sounds like it to me.

TARA: Well, I'm sure he's already forgotten me because remember I really liked him and he only "pretended" he liked me. So now maybe we're even.

JUSTIN: That's twisted.

TARA: You see? This whole thing just makes me crazy.

    (Pause.)

JUSTIN: It all happened so fast I don't even know what to think any more. I mean would it be such a big deal just to talk to him?

TARA: You do what you want, just leave me out of it.

    (TARA exits. After a beat JUSTIN exits. Transition music and ambient street sound are heard.)

Scene Fourteen

    (On the street. The transition music fades and we hear ambient street sounds. ANTONY and RACHEL enter.)

ANTONY: Come on girl, pull yourself together.

RACHEL: But it was so sad.

ANTONY: It's only a movie.

RACHEL: I know, but ...

    (CARL enters.)

ANTONY: Uh oh, here comes trouble.

CARL: Antony, can I talk to you for a sec?

RACHEL: Why? So you can insult him again?

CARL: Was I talking to you?

ANTONY: It's okay, Rachel.

CARL: Do you mind?

RACHEL: Call me if he starts giving you a hard time.

    (She exits.)

CARL: You know that thing that happened the other day ...

ANTONY: Look, it's okay, as long as we agree that we've got the right to disagree, it's cool.

CARL: All I meant was ...

ANTONY: Wouldn't life be easier for all of us if everyone acted straight?

CARL: Wouldn't it?

ANTONY: Sure, if I could've done that I would still be living at home. Unfortunately I couldn't act straight enough for a family of jocks but you can imagine how hard I tried. It was exhausting.

CARL: You still see them?

ANTONY: My family? Oyi—only when I have to. And if you can't accept me the way I am you know where you can stick it.

CARL: But if you could be straight ...

ANTONY: I'm happy the way I am.

CARL: But ...

ANTONY: I don't have a problem with who I am—been there, done that—if that's a problem for some people too bad for them. I figure as long as I'm not hurting anybody, people should mind their own business and I'll mind mine.

> *(Beat.)*

CARL: Did you always think you were ...?

ANTONY: It wasn't something I had to think about—you just know you are and you either accept it and get on with your life or you end up where you are.

CARL: And where's that?

ANTONY: I don't know exactly why you came to this program but I bet it's because somehow that closet door of yours was smashed open and people found out you weren't as straight as they thought you were. But you haven't really come out yet. You're still watching from the other side of the closet hoping that you can figure a way out. Trust me, girlfriend, there isn't.

CARL: See—like why do you have to call me "girlfriend"?

ANTONY: *(He puts on a macho act.)* "Oh right, sorry buddy. What'd ya say we go shoot some pool—down some brewskis—pick up a couple of chicks and beat up some fags?"

CARL: Been there, done that. *(Beat.)* Uh, what are you doing now?

ANTONY: Uh ... what do you mean?

CARL: A friend of mine's coming to pick me up any minute now and ... I was thinking ... You wanna hang out with us?

ANTONY: You're asking *moi*?

CARL: Sure ...

ANTONY: Well I don't know, my dance card is just about completely full ... oh hell, sure, why not, eh?

CARL: I've just got to go in and pick up my knapsack.

ANTONY: I'll be here.

> *(CARL exits. After a few beats PAULETTE enters looking for CARL. She exits. After a beat RICK enters.)*

RICK: Hey, do you know Carl Hunter?

ANTONY: Yeah, are you the friend he was expecting?

RICK: I don't think he's expecting me. So is this whole place full of fags?

ANTONY: Excuse me?

RICK: I heard Carl was going to some kind of special school or program or something and this is where it is, isn't it?

ANTONY: Maybe that's something you should be asking him.

RICK: It must be, because I've been watching people go in and out of here and they all look queer—like you.

ANTONY: Umm ... maybe I better go and see what's keeping Carl.

RICK: Why, are you his boyfriend?

ANTONY: Hey, who the hell are you?

>   *(RICK grabs ANTONY by his collar and begins to threaten him.)*

>   Let go of me.

RICK: What if I don't? You gonna scratch me with your nails?

>   *(CARL enters.)*

CARL: Okay, she should be here any second.

RICK: So this is where you've been hiding out, eh?

CARL: How did you get here?

RICK: I was curious who Paulette was sneaking off with.

CARL: You followed her?

ANTONY: Could you let me go now?

RICK: Am I making you nervous?

ANTONY: No, it's just that the last time I was this close to another guy we were slow dancing.

RICK: Watch your mouth, faggot—

CARL: Let him go—he's not the reason you came here.

>   *(RICK releases ANTONY.)*

RICK: So now you're a total fag, eh?

CARL: Why did you really come here?

RICK: I told you.

CARL: You're lying.

RICK: Huh?

CARL: Because you're scared—

RICK: Wha—

CARL: That's what's really been bugging you all along, isn't it?

RICK: What are / you—?

CARL: *(Overlapping.)* Scared because we messed around when we were twelve?

ANTONY: Uh oh.

CARL: You weren't scared / back then—

RICK: *(Overlapping.)* Shut up—

CARL: As I remember you were the one who / started it—

RICK: *(Overlapping.)* You're the one who's lying—

CARL: Am I? Just because you tried doesn't mean you're gay, Rick.

RICK: Nothing ever happened.

CARL: That's what you've been afraid of—that I would tell—

ANTONY: Come on Carl, let's go—

RICK: That never happened—

> *(PAULETTE enters.)*

ANTONY: Carl, you can get kicked out / of the program if they catch you fighting.

PAULETTE: *(Overlapping.)* What's going / on?

CARL: *(Overlapping.)* I don't care.

PAULETTE: What's he doing here?

CARL: He followed you.

ANTONY: This boy has some huge personal issues to work out, girlfriend. In fact if Carl wanted to he could go back to your school and tell everybody your little secret.

PAULETTE: What secret?

RICK: Nothing happened!

ANTONY: Hey, girlfriend, de-nial is not just a big river in Egypt.

> *(RICK jumps on ANTONY.)*

RICK: Shut up, faggot!

ANTONY: Get off me, you creep!

CARL: Leave him alone—I said leave him alone!

> *(CARL pulls RICK off ANTONY. CARL and RICK fight.)*

ANTONY: Guys—guys stop—

> *(CARL pins RICK down.)*

CARL: I'm not backing down any more you hear me?

PAULETTE: Carl, that's enough, let him up—

RICK: I'm going to kill you, you bastard—

ANTONY: Stop, man—he's had it—

(ANTONY and PAULETTE try to pull CARL off RICK. RICK slips loose and backs away. CARL quickly moves after him.)

PAULETTE: Call someone—go and get someone who can stop them—

ANTONY: But …

(CARL and RICK continue the fight off stage.)

PAULETTE: Do it!

(PAULETTE and ANTONY exit as we hear the sound of an ambulance siren. It transforms into the sound of someone running. Heart pumping. Gasping for breath. CARL appears in an isolated area.)

CARL: I can see him in front of me—running as fast as he can, but we both know I'm faster. He's within arm's reach, just like in my dream. He stumbles—falls—and my fists are pounding like jackhammers—wanting to hear those bones crush—wanting to see the pain and fear in his eyes—Rick's eyes—my fists just keep slamming away—at him—at me—Somewhere far away I can hear people yelling—trying to pull me away but the words in my head block them out. All the words jammed into my head until—

(Voice-overs: "Faggot, queer, homo, fairy," etc.—repeat until the end of the section.)

—whatever was left of me felt worthless—empty—until it was filled with hate …

"You bastard—Why couldn't you just leave me alone?!!" *(Beat.)* Then time stands still … I'm looking at a face I don't recognize covered in blood and I'm thinking … that could be me … Everything flows together after that … Paulette, Antony … the ambulance … the police …

(We hear the sound of a car motoring down a highway.)

Then I'm sitting in the car … Dad's driving—He hasn't looked at me since he picked me up … He can't … I could hear the embarrassment in his voice as he answered the questions … "No, my son doesn't have a history with violence …" How little you know, Dad, how little you know. Sorry I screwed up again. I don't seem to fit in anywhere, do I? I wish I could say something that could make you understand but the words won't form in my mouth. Can't find the words that will make me stop being a stranger in your eyes.

(We hear the sound of a phone ringing. We hear the voice-overs of JUSTIN and MARION.)

MARION: Hello?

CARL: The car engine is roaring in my ears ...

JUSTIN: Mrs. Hunter?

CARL: But there is silence between you and me that's deafening.

MARION: Who is this?

CARL: It's me! Carl! Remember me? Your son? Nothing's changed—I'm still here—

JUSTIN: Justin ... I just called ... is Carl there?

CARL: And the silence is like a thin sheet of ice that keeps getting thicker ...

MARION: No ...

JUSTIN: Well, will you tell him that I called? Ummm ... and that I talked to Rick's parents ... He's going to be okay.

MARION: Thank God ...

JUSTIN: And tell him ... umm ... I'll call back ...

(We hear a dial tone as CARL talks.)

CARL: I remember when I was a kid you used to say I had so much energy that if you and Mom weren't around to keep my feet on the ground I would fly to the moon and back before anyone even noticed I was missing ... remember?

(We hear the sound of a phone ringing.)

Fly to the moon ... that's what I'd like to do ... or maybe Mars ... or maybe just float in the endless vaccuum of space.

(We hear the voice-over of FRANK answering the phone.)

FRANK: Hello? Hello? Do you know what time it is?

CARL: Yeah, that's where I'd like to be. Floating free in the starry endless night where I wouldn't be weighed down by labels and rules that don't make sense to me any more.

FRANK: Your mother has been worried sick about you.

CARL: I'm just about to blast off, Dad. I've already started the count-down.

(The voice-overs of other characters bleed in.)

FRANK: I want you to come home right now—

CARL: Just thought I'd call and let you guys know I'll be all right ... I'll be thinking of you ...

RICK: Are you kidding? I don't have faggots for friends.

FRANK: Carl—listen to me—listen—

CARL: Ever wondered if you floated far enough out in space you might see heaven?

JUSTIN: Don't try and pretend you don't know what kind of bars are on Church Street.

FRANK: I know I haven't been dealing with this very well—

CARL: This is just going to make everything easier for everyone.

RICK: He never said anything about being queer.

FRANK: No, that wouldn't make / things easier—

CARL: *(Overlapping.)* I don't belong here / any more …

JUSTIN: Don't make him bleed, you could get AIDS.

FRANK: *(Overlapping.)* Of course you / belong …

TARA: My mother thinks it's against the will of God.

CARL: (/) No I don't—

FRANK: You're not listening / to me—

RICK: He's a fag …

CARL: (/) Just about time for takeoff … Ten …

FRANK: Will you just listen!

TARA: Maybe it's better for everyone that he's gone …

CARL: Nine …

FRANK: Son, I'm sorry …

JUSTIN: Forget that he ever existed …

CARL: Eight …

FRANK: For God's sake Carl—don't please—

CARL: Seven …

RICK: You want to fight me, faggot?

FRANK: I—I want you to come home …

PAULETTE: You're brave enough to go to a gay bar, but not to the dance?

CARL: Six …

PAULETTE: You've got just as much right to be there as anybody else.

FRANK: I'm willing to do whatever it takes to make this work, son …

CARL: Five …

ANTONY: Wouldn't life be easier for all of us if everyone acted straight?

FRANK: Whatever it takes—we'll work it out ...

CARL: Four ...

ANTONY: I'm happy the way I am.

FRANK: Carl, please ...

PAULETTE: You can't just give up.

CARL: Three ...

ANTONY: You either accept it and get on with your life or you end up where you are.

CARL: Two ...

FRANK: Come home ... just come home ...

CARL: There's only one way I'm coming home and it's this way ...

FRANK: Your mother and I love you, son ...

> *(CARL exits and we hear the sound of a phone dial tone. The end.)*

CHILE CON CARNE

BY
CARMEN AGUIRRE

Chile con Carne premièred at Station Street Arts Centre in Vancouver in October of 1995. It was sponsored by Norte-Sur Arts Association of the Americas, and was performed by the following cast:

MANUELITA	Carmen Aguirre
MOTHER's VOICE	Ana Duran
FATHER's VOICE	Pato Ibarra
PELAO's VOICE	Carlos Reygadas
FLACA's VOICE	Carmen Rodriguez

Directed and dramaturged by Guillermo Verdecchia
Set and costume design by Cecilia Boisier
Sound design by Alejandro Verdecchia
Lighting design by Michael Hirano
Production and stage manager: Michel Bisson
Promotion photography by Alejandra Aguirre
Slides by Tim Matheson
Paintings on poster and in slides by
Cecilia Boisier and Nora Patrich
Publicity by Helen Nestor

Chile con Carne was made possible thanks to financial assistance from the Canada Council for the Arts and the British Columbia Arts Council.

Characters

MANUELITA
MOTHER's VOICE
FATHER's VOICE
PELAO's VOICE
FLACA's VOICE

Setting

Vancouver, the mid 1970s.

(Seventies disco music has been playing through the walk-in. The stage is in darkness. There is a tree up stage right, a big trunk down stage right, and a child's school desk down stage left. There is a screen or sheet suspended on the back wall of the stage. The whole set—except for the tree—is painted like the sky, with hints of clouds.

The play begins with "The Prologue":

"Venceremos" by Inti-Illimani plays—or any other Inti-Illimani song celebrating Salvador Allende's rise to power. One verse of this celebratory song plays and is brutally interrupted by a huge bomb.

This is accompanied by a number of slides of Salvadore Allende and popular rallies in Chile during Allende's term. The bomb sound effect coincides with slides of the Presidential Palace in Santiago being bombed on September 11, 1973.

From the bomb, we go right into a small fragment of Allende's final speech, hours before his death. The part chosen is the one in which Allende talks about the great avenues being open once again in the future, where Chileans will walk freely. He then says, "Long live Chile, long live the working people, these are my last words ..." Allende's most famous words.

Throughout this section there are slides of Allende resisting at the Presidential Palace, with his helmet and rifle, surrounded by members of his government.

The titles for the different scenes of the play are projected onto the screen at the back of the stage; some titles are words, others just an image.

Slide: "Mom, Dad, and Friends Discuss Tactics in the Living Room."

Four adult voices—two men and two women—are heard talking very animatedly and loudly in Chilean Spanish.)

60

FATHER: No, pu compadres, la cuestión es, compadres, que los compañeros en Chile sepan que nosotros estamos super comprometidos con la causa, pu, compadres—

PELAO: Claro, pu huevón, por eso mismo yo propongo que hagamos una buena peña, pu huevón, completa con empanadas y unas buenas cumbias.

MOTHER: Yo estoy de acuerdo con el Pelao, ah, porque pucha a los gringos les gusta bailar salsa y a lo mejor un puro baile de salsa va a ser suficiente—

FLACA: Chucha, con que vengan los puros chilenos llenamos el Russian Hall, y mas con los gringos, puuu, a que llegan quinientas personas, y de paso hueveamos un rato y la pasamos bien, pu—

FATHER: Pero ustedes concha su madre, chucha pareciéra que sólo quieren revolverlas no mas, pu. Pero hay que comprobarle a los presos en Chile que nosotros apoyamas su huelga de hambre—

MOTHER: Pero no seai huevón. Yo no pienso hacer ninguna huelga de hambre—

FLACA: Yo tampoco, ah, mira que ya estoy más flaca que la cresta, ah—

FATHER: Y como creí que están los compañeros en Chile, que en la cárcel no les dan ni agua, pu, companera—

MOTHER: Oye, corta el huevéo. Lo que necesitamos hacer es juntar plata pa'a mandarles a las mujéres de los presos pa'a que puedan alimentar a los cabros chicos. La mejor manera es tener un baile de salsa y vender hartos tragos pa'a que los gringos tomen—

PELAO: Y hartas empanadas, pu comadre.

MOTHER: Ya, pu, hartas empanadas pa'a que los gringos coman harto también. No vamos a ganar na'a de plata haciendo una huelga de hambre acá en Canadá, pu huevón. Ademas, chi, que te creís? Quién va a cuidar a los cabros nuestros mientras nosotros nos matamos de hambre, concha su madre?

FATHER: Oye, si podemos ganar plata, pu huevona. Una huelga de hambra causaría sensación acá en Canadá. Tú que tanto te preocupai por los gringos, ya pu, tu creís que los gringos no van a donar plata cuando vean un montón de Chilenos en la United Church haciendo una huelga de hambra en solidaridad con los presos políticos en Chile? Chucha, si a los gringos se les cae la baba por huevadas asi. Va a llegar la tele, los diarios, las radios, y los compadres en Chile van a saber que no nos estamos puro rascando las hue'as—Ademas la plata que se done se manda directo a las familias de los presos—

PELAO: Oiga compadre entiendo su propuesta pero la comadre tiene razón, pu. Que hacemos con nuestros cabros chicos?

FLACA: Chucha, que me están aburriendo hasta las hueva'as, porqué no hacemos las dos cuestiones no mas? Baile de salsa y huelga de hambre, y a propósito hay una galla que es súper buena artista y que se ofreció pa'a hacer los posters de "Boycott Chilean Goods"—

(Moments after the discussion starts, subtitles in English flash on the screen at the back of the stage. This is what each slide should say:

1. "We want our comrades in Chile to know that we are very committed to the cause."

2. "Yeah. We should have a big benefit party with lots of empanadas *and good music."*

3. "Yeah. Gringos love to dance salsa."

4. "No. We have to do a hunger strike."

5. "Don't be a dick. I'm not gonna do a hunger strike."

6. "Me neither. I'm skinny enough as it is."

7. "Listen. We need to make money. The best way is to have a big dance and sell lots of booze and lots of empanadas.*"*

8. "We won't make any money doing a hunger strike."

9. "Yes, we will. The gringos will donate money for a bunch of Chileans doing a hunger strike at the United Church. Gringos love shit like that. And the comrades in Chile will know we're not just sitting around scratching our balls and we'll send all the money we raise directly to the families of political prisoners."

10: "Shit. Why don't we just do both. Why don't we have a salsa dance and a hunger strike."

Mixed in with the subtitles, there will also be a slide of an empanada *and some wine.*

The voices are very loud and very animated. It is very important that the actors chosen to record the voices be Chilean, in order to capture the accent and intonation. There should be no pauses in the adults' discussion; they are continually interrupting one another.When MOTHER is saying, "Don't be a dick," MANUELITA comes running in. She listens to her parents, decides that their conversation is boring, and goes directly to the trunk. She opens it and it spills over with "dress-ups": old slips and nightgowns and a few old, matted blonde wigs of different lengths.

MANUELITA is wearing her hair in two braids that stick out of the side of her head—not straight out like Pippi Longstocking, just out—with a part in the middle. She wears bell-bottomed barf-coloured corduroy pants that are too short, black patent leather shoes with frilly pink socks, and a red polyester T-shirt that says "Disneyland" on it. MANUELITA is eight years old.

MANUELITA checks out the dress-ups and finally decides to wear only a blonde wig for today, no dress-ups. She listens to her parents again, decides that they're still boring, and leaves the house. MANUELITA should leave as FLACA finishes saying, "Boycott Chilean goods." The voices cut out abruptly. MANUELITA climbs her tree and starts eating her "Tang" straight out of the package.

Slide: a child's drawing of a tree.

MANUELITA eats her tang and watches the passers-by. She looks out into the audience and realizes she is being watched. She offers the audience some Tang.)

MANUELITA: This is Cedar. I found him a year ago. The day after we got here. There's no trees like Cedar in Valparaíso. There's all these tractors here and gringos too. They're all down there. They're chopping all the trees down. I think they wanna make a house here. I don't care what they do to the other trees. As long as they don't chop Cedar down.

I come here every day after school to have my snacks and watch the passers-by. This is where I read the letters from my grandma and Gabriela. Nobody knows about Cedar. Not even Joselito. He's like my cousin.

(MANUELITA climbs down the tree and goes to the desk.

The title of this section is a slide of a can of chili con carne. "Oh, Canada" plays as MANUELITA stands by her desk. As the anthem plays, MANUELITA hangs on to her crotch, desperate to pee. When the anthem is over, she sits at her desk.)

(To the audience.) Everyone at school thinks I'm mute. So they always say things to me, 'cause they know I'm not gonna talk back. "Fuck you, bitch," and "Hey, Speedy González, why don't you speedy back home," and "You're from Chile, chili con carne."

So today is just another mute day for me. Same as always. Miss Mitten goes from desk to desk helping kids out with their reading, and I'm sitting really still, with my legs crossed like a señorita, 'cause I really have to go pee but I don't know how to say it, when all of a sudden somebody brings their desk over and sits beside me!

It's the beautiful honey-coloured girl! Honey eyes, honey freckles, honey skin, honey hair. She's wearing French-cut jeans and her lunch-kit has Charlie's Angels on it! She's smiling at me with her really shiny braces, and she even has a watch! And little pearl earrings!

"Rrrr Leslie. Rrrr?"

"Lassie."

"*Les*lie."

"Lassie."

"*Leslie*. L-E-S-L-I-E."

(Slide: Lassie, the dog.)

Her name is Lassie! I remember in Chile I used to watch Lassie on TV. I didn't know any dogs like Lassie in Chile. All the dogs I used to know had scabies and ran around the neighbourhood in packs.

My friend Lassie is talking and talking still and pointing at the door. She looks at my crotch. We look at my crotch. She wants to take me to the bathroom 'cause I peed my pants.

(The title of this section is a slide of two little girls playing on a dirt road in Chile.

MANUELITA faints. The "Faint" song plays throughout the next section. This is a spooky composition by the sound designer.)

The floor opens up and sucks me in and back, back to the kitchen in Valparaíso when I would help my grandmother make the *empanadas*, back to the lane where me and Gabriela would swap necklaces made of watermelon seeds, back to the plaza where we got our picture taken with the white donkey full of decorations— I wonder if that picture's still sitting on my grandmother's piano?

Caballito blanco llévame de aquí, llévame a mi pueblo donde yo nací, tengo tengo tengo tu no tienes nada …

(MANUELITA gets up from the floor.

The title of this section is a slide of a Colonia Inglesa bottle.)

Me and Lassie are punished. Miss Mitten said we have to stay after school 'cause we were bad. So we're cleaning the cloakroom 'cause Miss Mitten told us to, when I see my dad poke his head in! I run up to him and he picks me up and twirls me around and hugs and kisses me, *"Mi niña linda, mi reina preciosa, qué pasó, se volvió a mear la niñita, pero mijita, es cuestión de pedir permiso pa'a ir al baño, no más, pucha, si no va a vivir meada la pobre, y se paspa …"* My dad smells like Colonia Inglesa, he smells like my grandfather and my uncles and all the men in Chile, and that smell, that smell is sad, so sad, but I don't know why.

I remember Lassie, she must think I'm a baby. I tell my dad to put me down right away. I tell him this is my new friend Lassie. My dad laughs and goes to give her a hug and a kiss, but she takes some steps back and shakes her head. My dad still doesn't understand that gringos don't really touch that much. I'm about to tell him that when I see Lassie's mother come in!

She's really tall and skinny with long blonde hair and sunglasses. She's wearing high-heeled clogs and bell-bottom jeans with a white shirt. She's got really long red nails with diamond rings! She's smoking a cigarette.

My dad says, "Jorge González." She says her name and doesn't even shake my dad's hand, she just blows smoke in his face and won't even take off her glasses. She says something to Lassie and starts to leave. Lassie is gathering her stuff and leaving too. She says something to me and waves goodbye.

Me and my dad are outside. We're pushing the car and some boys from grade seven are helping. We always have to push our car. It's really big and smells like a basement. My dad found it and him and his friends fixed it a bit.

Lassie and her mom are sitting in their car. It's a big pink convertible and it's shiny and new! Her mom is still smoking and bobbing her head up and down, and Lassie's talking and talking. Finally Lassie comes running out of her car, right to me! She takes my arm and pulls me to her car and she talks and talks. She's really excited! My dad says, "I think she wants you to go visit her!" Wow! Lassie's house! Wow! I've never been to anybody's house here, only to the Chileans', and those don't count. I wonder if her house will be just like the ones on TV! Maybe her house will be like the ones my mother cleans! She says people here have so much money, they throw food in the garbage, and clothes and fridges and furniture—that's where we get our stuff, my mom brings it from the big houses.

My dad has walked up to Lassie's car and he's waving his arms and acting things out for Lassie's mom. He only speaks Spanish, so he has to wave his arms a lot. Lassie's mom just nods and smokes.

My dad says that it's okay. I can go visit Lassie and he'll pick me up before dinner. He got directions and everything. He gives me a hug and a kiss and Lassie takes me to her car. I get in the back seat.

(Slide: "Manuelita Discovers America."

Rod Stewart's "Do You Think I'm Sexy" begins to play.)

Lassie's mom is playing the music really loud! She screeches off. She drives just like Charlie's Angels! I look back and see my dad, with all the boys, still pushing the car, he looks up and waves. I watch him get further and further away. Before I know it, we're in a neighbourhood I've never seen before. The houses look like the wedding cakes at the store we clean at night, and the sidewalks are so clean even my grandmother would be impressed. I smile and bob my head up and down to the music, just like Lassie's mom. This is my first North American experience. And I am alone.

"This is María," says Lassie. She's a lady that looks like my mother. She's wearing a black dress and an apron. She speaks to me in Spanish. She sounds different. María says she's from Mexico. She says that Lassie told her about me, so Lassie brought me here to meet her. María asks me what part of Mexico I'm from. I say I'm not from Mexico. I'm from Chile. María laughs and says that Lassie thought I was from Mexico. My throat's got a big knot in it. María's really nice. But I hate her. I wish she would die. María put my pants and undies in the washer. I'm wearing one of Lassie's pants for now. Lassie's mother has disappeared and me and Lassie are having pink milk and cookies. Just like on TV. Lassie's talking and talking to me and María's polishing silver in the living room. The knot in my throat is getting smaller, so I can swallow my pink milk easy.

Lassie keeps talking and she gets up. I follow her. We go up these big huge stairs and she takes me to a door. She opens it and I see the most beautiful sight in the whole wide world! Lassie's room is full of big white shelves and shelves and shelves of dolls! Some are dolls with soothers and pink dresses! Some come with little baby carriages! They're the most beautiful dolls in the world! Then, I see them! A huge shelf full of Barbies! Barbies! The Barbies have cars and houses and jeeps and swimming pools and all these shoes and clothes and purses and mini-lipsticks and neck-laces! I run from shelf to shelf, *"Mira ésta! Y ésta! Qué linda! Me puedes regular una, Lassie? Juguemos con ésta! No! Con ésta! Con las dos! Mira! Mira! Te pasaste, Lassie, te pasaste!"* Lassie's laughing. I'm speaking Spanish and she doesn't understand me.

I hear my dad's voice downstairs. He's talking really loud, like he always does. He's talking in Spanish with María. Lassie says something and laughs, then she says *"Arriba arriba, andale, andale."* She points at me and laughs. I just laugh too.

(MANUELITA lies on her back.

Slide: Cecilia Boisier's painting of women running with suit-cases. Throughout this section we will see numerous slides of Boisier's paintings of people fleeing.

We hear the sounds of military raiding a house with "Misa Criolla" by Ariel Ramírez playing underneath.)

Sometimes at night my dad screams in his sleep. He yells out, "No, no!" and my mom has to shake him awake. My mom told me he has dreams at night that the military's going to get him. I remember in Valparaíso when I came from school and they were in the house, checking everything. They were even in the closets.

So now I always check the bathtub before I go pee, just in case there's a military still in there. Even though my mom explained that they're not in Canada. That day, they took my dad away and my mom and grandma were crying. My dad didn't come back.

A whole year later me, my mom, and my grandma went to Santiago in El Italiano's taxi. My mom and my grandma cried the whole time and our suitcases were on the roof. I was wearing the pink dress that Auntie Cuqui made for me and my grandma had curled my hair. We got to the airport and I looked for my dad everywhere 'cause my mom said he'd be there waiting for us. But I didn't see him. Finally we got on the big plane and we saw my dad. He looked different. He was really skinny. My mom climbed on him in front of everybody and my dad hugged her with his one arm. The other hand was handcuffed to the airplane seat. But that was already a long time ago. Almost a year. But my dad still has bad dreams.

(MANUELITA goes to Cedar and climbs it.)

I went to Lassie's house again. María made us these really funny Canadian sandwiches and Lassie taught me how to say them: "Peanut butter and banana."

The tractor people are down there. They're eating and burping like gringos do. There's some fancy gringos all gathered around a thing like a map. They keep pointing right at Cedar.

("Trabajadores al Poder" by Karaxu begins to paly. MANUELITA hears it, climbs down from her tree, and goes to her trunk. She puts on a pink nightgown.

Slide: a poster that says, "An active resistance demands an active solidarity.")

Trabajadores trampolé, trabajadores trampolé . . . we're gonna go to a *peña* tonight. That's like a benefit party. My mom and dad and their friends planned everything. We're going to the Ukrainian Hall in Chinatown. My mom said I could dress up, even though it's snowing outside.

(A cueca *by Victor Jara begins to play and MANUELITA crosses over to her desk. She sits on top of it.)*

We had to pick up Juan of the Chickens on the way here. We call him that because he works at a chicken restaurant. He has to wear a chicken costume. He has to be outside the restaurant and run around, pretending to be a chicken. Sometimes we go visit him and I can see his eyes through the beak. Today he was being a chicken outside the restaurant, but he still doesn't realize it gets slippery when it snows, so he slipped and fell. He twisted his ankle. So that's why we went to pick him up.

("La Colegiala" by Rodolfo y Su Típica begins to play. MANUELITA gets up.)

Oye! Juan! Baila conmigo! Ya pu!

(MANUELITA dances with JUAN.)

Now Juan of the Chickens is drinking some wine even though he's not allowed to here 'cause he's only seventeen, and he's saying it's too bad we have to boycott the Chilean kind 'cause this one tastes like shit. Juan of the Chickens arrived just a few months ago. He ran away from the jail in Valparaíso and snuck on a ship. Then they made him get off in Squamish 'cause they found him. He was really skinny and full of burns and bruises. So my mom and dad and their friends had to help him. He was taking care of me once 'cause my mom and dad were busy and he showed me a picture of his girlfriend in Valparaíso . *La Chueca* he calls her, 'cause her legs go like this. He says he's gonna bring her here and I can teach her English. Juan of the Chickens is real excited about La Chueca coming here. He tells me how he writes long letters to her, describing the apartments here, with carpets and fridges and electric stoves and central heating. He tells me this with his eyes wide open, like this.

"Puta, pu, Manuelita. Si vivimos como reyes acá y quiero que la Chueca lo vea, pu."

He never thought he'd be in a country where all you have to do to furnish your house is go through the alleys, and you can even find cars and just fix them. He says he found a white leather couch already and fixed it up, for when La Chueca comes. Juan of the Chickens keeps talking and finally he stops.

"Manuelita, why are you looking at me like that?"

"'Cause I thought you were gonna go back to Chile, with everybody else."

"What are you talking about, little one? No one's going back to Chile for a long long time."

"Yes, they are! We are! My mom and dad always say we're going back really soon! As soon as he falls!

(A slide of Pinochet comes on at this point.)

"No, Manuelita. Your mom and dad are on the blacklist, and they're not allowed back in. And he won't fall for a long long time."

My stomach hurts, like he's hit me right in the tummy. I can't breathe. I can't talk. He's a liar, he's a liar, he's a fucking liar. My mom always says we never get any furniture 'cause we're leaving next month, as soon as he falls, she always says, the revolution will come and he will fall, he will fall, that's why we have to work hard, to make him fall, that's why you can't forget Manuelita don't ever forget, you are one hundred percent Chilean, Manuelita. Don't ever forget. You are a mix of Basque blood and Mapuche blood. Don't forget. Don't speak that ugly language, Manuelita, speak Spanish, speak Spanish, you are not Canadian, so don't even try it, speak your language, Manuelita, *now!!* I run away to the bathroom.

(Slide: a porcelain doll with the head torn off.

MANUELITA runs to centre stage and lands on the floor, face down.)

I remember my toys sitting on the dresser in Chile, waiting. The porcelain doll passed all the way down from my great-grandmother. The clown with the drum. The table and chairs my father made for me.

My mom comes into the bathroom. She tries to hug me, but I won't let her. I want to say "Hey, Speedy González, why don't you speedy back home," but all I can do is kick.

(MANUELITA gets up from the floor.)

Quiero a mi abuelita! I want my grandma! I see my mother leaning against the wall. I see her hands, swollen from washing too many dishes, one over her mouth, the other against the wall. She's got two bandages, she cut herself making the five hundred *empanadas* for the *peña.* She lets herself slide down the wall, and rocks back and forth, *"Ay, Dios mío, ayúdame, Dios mío, por favor,"* she says it over and over again. I hear her do this sometimes, but she's never done it in front of me, until now.

"What's the blacklist?"

She gets herself up from the floor and starts to wash her face.

"What's the blacklist?"

"It means your passport is marked."

(MANUELITA walks over to the desk and sits on top of it.)

We drive home from the *peña*. It's four in the morning, and the streets are deserted.

(The title of this section is a slide of a Chinese store sign.)

It's snowing in Chinatown and the heater in the car doesn't work, my dad has to keep slowing down to wipe the foggy window. My mom is silent.

(A slide of a neon Chinese restaurant sign replaces the former one.)

I see a Chinese sign. "You wanna hear the song Lassie taught me today? … Chinese Japanese, dirty knees, look at these, money please."

(MANUELITA slaps her face.)

"Cállate, cabra 'e mierda. Don't you ever say that again. Don't you dare. We're just like them, Manuela del Carmen González Mancilla. We're just like them. We're not like the gringos here, we're like other the immigrants. Don't you dare turn against your own kind."

My father's trying to explain, "That's racist, Manuelita. Very racist. Someday you'll understand."

My parents are going on and on about how I'm turning into a gringa already, that we have to go back as soon as possible, that I'm forgetting who I am, this business about wearing the wigs has gone too far, that I want to be a gringa.

How can I tell them that I do? That I would do anything to be a gringa, to have long blonde hair and sparkling blue eyes, to be called Sherry or Sandy, to have David MacWilliams who's in grade four pay attention to me at least once, to be called pretty rather than spic or weirdo or bitch? I would do anything, to have my parents and all their friends understand me … I would do anything for a Barbie.

"Since we're on the blacklist and all my dolls are in Chile, can I get a Barbie?"

"Who told you we're on the blacklist?"

"Juan of the Chickens told her. He said he was sorry, he didn't know she didn't know."

"Don't worry, Manuelita. We won't be on the blacklist for long. We're gonna go on a hunger strike till they take us off."

"You idiot. You weren't supposed to tell her yet. Now she's gonna keep pissing her pants in school. Manuelita, we are going to go on a hunger strike, but not for a while. You can see us every day, and then we'll be off the blacklist and we can go back, Grandma says it's not so bad any more in Chile—"

"I just wanna know if I can get a Barbie!!"

"Okay, Manuelita, okay. We'll get you a doll."

"A Barbie!!"

"A Barbie."

The memory of the setting sun over the Valparaíso fades in the neon signs that flash as we drive through the snow.

("My Sharona" by The Knack begins to play. MANUELITA goes to her trunk, gets rid of the pink nightgown and dances in front of her mirror, practicing being "Canadian.")

Gawd, you guys. Gawd. Gross. You think you're so great. You guys! You punker. You punker. Show off, show off, nuthin' but a show off.

(MANUELITA pulls at her T-shirt, imagining she has breasts. She checks out her ass.)

Hi, David.

(She runs to Cedar and climbs it.

Slide: a tree being chopped down.)

I know Cedar's next. He's the only one left standing. I finally decided to tell Joselito about Cedar and the critical situation.

(MANUELITA starts tying a bandana around her face.)

Joselito said the only way to proceed was armed struggle since you can't have a dialogue with the enemy. Juan of the Chickens was an urban guerilla in Valparaíso so we got some pointers from him.

Tonight's the night. Joselito slept over and we're gonna break the windows on the tractors.

(MANUELITA takes out a huge kitchen knife and holds it up to her left index finger.)

But first we become blood brothers.

(The stage goes black, we hear windows breaking. As the lights come up, we hear the sound of birds chirping. MANUELITA is

reading out a letter she has written. Her left index finger has a huge white bandage on it.

Slide: a child's letter with a drawing of a snowman and a sled.

The "Letter" song, an original composition by the sound designer that should sound like a fairy tale, plays softly underneath the letter.)

Querida Abuelita:

Estoy aprendiendo a bailar la cueca and disco too. At lunch I go to disco dancing classes, Grandma, I wish you were here or I was there so I could show you my steps.

Here everything's okay. My dad works really hard at a paper kind of factory, he even has to work all night sometimes, and me and my mom clean a bakery and a hair salon at night. My mom cleans rich people's houses during the day. She brings home nice clothes that they give her.

We have a lot of friends from Chile, Grandma. There's Fiaca, who used to be a psychologist and now she works at a hotel, and there's Guatón, who used to be a journalist and now he has two paper routes and he works sometimes at a weiner factory, and lots of others.

At school I made a good friend called Lassie, just like the dog, she's very nice and very pretty, maybe you can meet her sometime. I'm sending you a drawing of *El Parque de Estanli:* Stanley Park. That's me in the middle. I'm on a sled.

Send many hugs and kisses to everybody in the neighbourhood, especially Gabriela. I love you, Abuelita.

Manuelita.

(MANUELITA puts the letter in an envelope and takes it with her as she slowly walks towards the desk. Music resembling the sound of a heartbeat plays, composed by the sound designer.

Slide: the southern cone of South America.)

At school nobody knows I dance *cueca.* Nobody knows I work at the bakery and at the hair salon. Nobody knows my house is always full of my parents' friends having meetings till really late. Nobody knows we have protests and rallies, nobody knows we have *peñas* and salsa dances, nobody knows my parents are going on a hunger strike. Nobody knows my dad was in jail. Nobody knows we're on the blacklist. Nobody from school, not even Lassie, comes over to my house. Nobody knows we have posters of Fidel Castro and Ché Guevara on the walls. Nobody knows about the Chilean me at school.

(MANUELITA arrives at the desk.

Slide: a Mountie smiling down at a blonde boy.)

The man from the RCMP is here to talk about safety. So stupid!

(MANUELITA sits down at the desk.)

He's a *huge* gringo policeman, with a gun at his side! I bet he knows that me and Joselito broke the windows on the tractors and now he's come to get me. Then I'll be in jail. Just like my dad was. He's standing at the front of the class with a nice warm smile on his face. "Hi, kids," he says. I remember those nice grins, those are the same grins they wore when they raided our house and they tore my favourite doll's head off. I sit in the first row of desks so I can see the gun real clearly. It's real all right, but it's smaller than the ones in Chile. The man starts talking about dangerous men in the woods and never get in cars and never take money from strangers, but I'm thinking, I know. I know what you're really about. My mom explained to me once that the gringos helped to do the coup in Chile, that's why we always have protests outside the U.S. consulate, so I know what you're up to, mister. You're trying to get us to trust you, but "No, sir." He takes his gun out slowly and holds it like this, flat in his hands, he's talking about how he never uses it, when all of a sudden I hear a kid screaming real loud. A few moments go by before I realize it's me that's screaming.

(MANUELITA stands on the desk and does a silent scream, turning in a circle. She does a full circle and climbs down, staring down at the seat.)

There's a puddle of pee on my seat. Miss Mitten comes up to me with a frozen smile and eyes that are about to pop out. She hits me on the head with her flashcards.

(MANUELITA runs to Cedar.)

I can hear the kids laughing 'cause I peed, but I run all the way home and here, to Cedar.

(MANUELITA climbs up Cedar.)

Juan of the Chickens explained that to be an urban guerilla you must use different tactics for your strategy. It's not all just molotov cocktails and burning trees for barricades.

(MANUELITA takes the petition that's hanging on a nail from the tree.)

So me and Joselito started this petition. We used my dad's Spanish–English dictionary to write it, then Bill, our friend from the refugee hotel, corrected it. Bill's a gringo, and he's the leader of the gringos' solidarity group and Flaca is in love with him. I can tell by the way she looks at him when she puffs on her cigarette. But Flaca can't do anything with Bill 'cause she's married to Pelao. But I saw Bill and Flaca in the back yard once. Me and Joselito were spying on them. Shame shame double shame, now I know your boyfriend's name.

I've already got a whole page of signatures. Even María and Mr. Singh, the janitor from school, signed it. Joselito's got two pages already. But that's okay, 'cause my mom explained that when you're fighting for a cause you shouldn't compete with your comrades. After we've got all the signatures, our final tactic will be a big protest right by Cedar.

("La Batea" by Quilapayun begins to play. MANUELITA hears it and walks over to the trunk. She pulls out a sign that says "Get Your Dirty Hands Off Cedar."

Slide: a sign that says "Boycott Chilean Goods.")

We're staying up late tonight, making these signs, 'cause tomorrow we're gonna protest outside of Safeway, 'cause they sell Chilean fruit.

(MANUELITA takes the sign and a marker centre stage and works on her sign.)

Joselito and me are taking this opportunity to make signs for the protest we're gonna have by Cedar. Lassie says she'll come protest too. She's never been to a protest so she's kind of excited. Everybody's here tonight: all the Chileans, and all the gringos too. The Chileans used to make fun of the gringos 'cause they dress funny, but my mom told the Chileans to shut the fuck up because the gringos had a big heart and were willing to do solidarity with a country they'd never even been to.

(MANUELITA puts the sign and the marker back in the trunk and sits on the trunk.)

But the gringos do dress kind of funny. They have different-coloured hair and stuff. My mom explained that they're from a thing called the Anarchist Movement, and the hippy ones are draft-dodgers she called them, from the U.S., and then she said that some are also from the Gay and Lesbian Movement. My dad got kinda red when she explained what gays and lesbians are, but she told him to grow up so he didn't say anything. Ever since she explained what they were, I don't make Barbie and Ken kiss at Lassie's house. I practice with two Barbies kissing, it doesn't look so bad.

(MANUELITA stands up, opens the trunk, and starts putting the pink nightgown on again.)

I'm getting ready 'cause me, my mom, and Crespa are going to buy me a Barbie. Today is the first time we go to a store that's not the Salvation Army, even though lately we've been going to the Army and Navy, but that doesn't count, 'cause only immigrants go there. Today we're actually going to a mall, and my mom says we're gonna have lunch at McDonald's. Yay! I already know exactly which Barbie I want: The one with hair down to her knees. Her hair's kinda wavy, and she comes dressed with an evening gown and gold shoes. I already know what I'm gonna call her too. Marsha. Marsha.

(At the mall.)

We find the aisle with all the Barbies on the shelves, just like at Lassie's house, and I see the one I want. I take her and study her closely. When I look up, my mom is holding a Barbie too. She walks up to me with it and says, "This one's perfect for you, Manuelita." Crespa's standing behind her, smiling.

(MANUELITA faints. The "Faint" song comes on.)

The floor opens up and sucks me in, and down, down to the place where I go to as I lie awake at night, and my mind speaks to me in English. The world spins and my grandmother's face turns into a blur. I land in the schoolyard where I speak only English. In Lassie's house where I speak only English. The floor sucks me away from all this Chilean-ness.

(MANUELITA gets up from the floor.)

I look at the Barbie my mother has chosen: a Hawaiian dancer, complete with grass skirt and flower necklace. "Look, she's beautiful, Manuelita, just like you," says my mom, and she holds the Barbie up to my arm, "And she's got your skin colour." Crespa says, "You can call her María or Carmen." No Marsha. I have a knot in my throat now so I can't speak. I put Marsha back and walk to the cashier with the Hawaiian dancer. Marsha's skin was the colour of snow. This Barbie's skin, my skin, is the colour of shit.

("Island Girl" by Elton John begins to play.

MANUELITA takes off the pink nightgown and throws it into the trunk. She pulls the Hawaiian dancer Barbie out of the trunk and some white nail polish. She paints the Barbie's leg white, becomes frustrated with the results and starts to paint her own arm and hand white. She realizes this is not going to work, so she throws the Barbie and nail polish back into the trunk.

MANUELITA walks centre stage.)

We all decided to do a big barbecue at Cates Park so everybody could celebrate and eat like pigs before the hunger strike. The Chileans are trying to teach Bill and the other gringos *cueca*, while I try and teach Joselito the hustle, that I learned yesterday at disco dancing classes.

(MANUELITA does a few steps from the hustle.)

Joselito points and I see Crespa sneaking into the woods with Cachete, even though she's married to Titicaco. Crespa and Cachete sitting in a tree, k-i-s-s-i-n-g! First comes love, then comes marriage, then comes Crespa and the baby carriage!

There's a big group of people next to us. They don't speak English either, and my mom explains that they're from India and to stop staring. They're kinda loud. Just like us. I hear lots of noise, and I see a big group of Canadians coming. They got here on motor-cycles, and all the ladies are wearing tight jeans and feathered hair, like Farrah Fawcett. They look nice. They set up their stuff and start looking at the people from India. They look and laugh and point. Some of them plug their noses and one of the men from India starts yelling at the Canadians, he's about to go and hit him, when all the other Indian men grab him and hold him back. The Canadians keep laughing, and now all the men are on their feet. I'm starting to feel sick, the hairs on the back of my neck rise and my knees are wobbly. Next thing I know, all the Chileans walk over to join the Indian people. Pelao is really mad, he starts swearing at the Canadians, "You kitchens! Kitchens! Kitchens! Kitchens!" and finally the Canadians leave.

(MANUELITA sits on top of the desk.)

For the rest of the day, we let the people from India taste our food and we taste theirs, and they dance for us and we dance for them and everybody looks really happy, but all I feel is a big black emptiness, right here. And it hasn't gone away yet.

(MANUELITA walks over to Cedar and climbs it. The "Letter" song plays throughout.

Slide: a child's spelling test. MANUELITA takes the clipboard and begins to write.)

Querida Abuelita:

Ahora ya sé bailar el Car Wash, it's a disco dance, I wish I could show you the steps, grandma. The other day we had a protest in front of the Chilean consulate and we let all the balloons go into the air and now all the adults are going on a hunger strike, but you don't have to worry 'cause they're gonna have a doctor check them every day. I wish I could go on the hunger strike but I'm too small and besides I have to go to school. I'm sending you my last spelling test. The gold star means that all my answers are right. I speak English good now but I still speak Spanish. Send hugs to all my aunts and uncles and cousins, and to Gabriela too, even though I haven't answered her last letter. Oh, well.

I love you, Abuelita,

Manuelita.

("Cancion de los C.D.R." by Silvio Rodríguez begins to play and MANUELITA goes and stands on the trunk.

Slide: a protest in Chile by the Mothers of the Disappeared.)

Vomité, vomité, vomité... Today's the first day of the hunger strike and everybody's here. There's even some First Nations people beating on a drum to show their solidarity with us. The TV is here. All the Chileans are dressed real nice 'cause they're gonna be on TV, and Bill's gonna translate for everybody. Pelao's already talking about how hungry he is and the hunger strike hasn't started yet and Juan of the Chickens keeps talking about how sick he is of eating fried chicken and Calladita keeps elbowing him in the ribs, 'cause he's not supposed to talk about food in front of the strikers. My mom and dad are being interviewed. My father's face lights up for the camera, and Bill can barely keep up with the translating ... We are here because we want the world to know that the Chilean people haven't laid down to die, that in spite of the unbridled murder, torture, and disappearances being carried out now against our *compañeros*, we, the exiles, continue to fight for our country, even from outside ... My father's old voice, the one from before, comes to life and that old sparkle, the one he lost after the coup, the one that died when we came here, explodes into his eyes. His back straightens, his hands fly like birds and his smile shines like a piano. There is absolute silence as my father continues. I walk up to him, put an arm around his leg and my hand in his. I can smell his Colonia Inglesa, I can smell the *mil hojas* cake my grandmother made to bid us farewell, I can smell the diesel in the Alameda! I would give anything, anything, *anything* to go back now, maybe I can erase the marks on my parents' passports and nobody will notice. Maybe Joselito can help me, it will be our secret operation and we'll be blood brothers again for it.

("A Cochabamba Me Voy," by Victor Jara begins to play.

Slide: a young Nicaraguan woman with a rifle slung on her shoulder. She's nursing a baby.

MANUELITA climbs onto the desk and plays at being a guerilla fighter: she looks around, ducks, hides, and so on.)

Juan of the Chickens is telling us all about Tania, the guerilla, Ché's right-hand woman in Bolivia.

(MANUELITA runs to the trunk and crouches by it.)

He's acting everything out for us as Calladita laughs and shakes her head.

(MANUELITA sits on the trunk.)

Juan of the Chickens and Calladita are in charge of all us kids during the hunger strike. We're all in our pyjamas and it's late. Every night Juan of the Chickens and Calladita take turns teaching us about the history of our people, they call it. They also teach us Spanish writing and reading 'cause we're kinda forgetting and they make us dance the *cueca* too. Then all us kids sleep in my room and Calladita sleeps in my parents' room and Juan of the Chickens in the living room. Tonight me and Joselito are gonna do another big operation. We're gonna wait till Calladita's asleep, then we're gonna sneak into my parents' room and take their passports. They're in the bottom dresser drawer.

(MANUELITA lies on the trunk.)

So me and Joselito are in my room. We make sure the other kids are asleep.

(MANUELITA crawls up stage left and stays there, on her knees.)

Then we crawl out of my room, into the hall and creep right into my parents' room. We can hear Juan of the Chickens snoring and talking in his sleep in the living room. We can't hear anything from Calladita, so we assume she's as quiet when she's sleeping as when she's awake. Joselito stands guard while I go through the drawer.

(Slide: the cover of a Chilean passport.)

I find the passports real easy.

(MANUELITA crawls up stage right and stays on her knees.)

We sneak into the bathroom, climb into the bathtub, and close the curtain. Joselito lights a match so I can look for the marks. I have no idea what these marks are supposed to look like—

(Slide: the inside of the passport with a big "L" scrawled across it.)

They're huge! They take up a whole page. It will take many nights' work to get rid of these marks, but we're willing to do it. Phase one of our operation is done.

(MANUELITA gets up from the floor and walks to the desk. She sits in it.)

I told Lassie that me and Joselito are urban guerillas. She promised not to tell anybody but then she got real excited so we started up our own urban guerilla group at school. We carry out secret operations.

(Slide: "If You Go Into the Woods Today.")

Me and Lassie recruited Catherine Suzanne and Yoko and Megan and Rashmi and a couple of other girls in the class. We decided our first operation would be to try and find the bad men in the woods that the policeman was talking about that day I pissed myself and screamed and ran away.

(The sound of a buzzer.

MANUELITA goes down stage centre and drags herself along the floor, crossing up stage centre.)

It's lunch time and we're all sneaking into the woods. We drag ourselves along the ground until we're finally in the forbidden zone.

(MANUELITA stands up.)

Today we're gonna try and make it down to the ravine, 'cause we'll find lots of clues down there and the bad men might be hiding there. The other girls nod. "Here's a clue," says Lassie. She holds up a twig for us all to inspect. "I bet the bad men stepped on it," I say, following Lassie's train of thought. All the other girls nod. I decide to keep this clue, so I put it in my pocket and we continue on our way. We find some scratches on a rock, and we realize the bad men must have sharpened their knives on it. We know we're getting close. They must be very near. We're gonna write the bad men a note and leave it hanging on this tree, just so they know they're dead. The others nod.

"Who's gonna write the note?" asks Yoko. It has to be someone who has boy's handwriting, so the bad men won't know it's us who wrote it. None of us has boy's handwriting, but Megan is the best choice 'cause she can fake the squiggliness of it really good. She writes: "Beware, bad men. We're gonna get you," and then she draws a skull. We hang the note on a tree right on the edge of the ravine.

(The sound of a buzzer.)

Lunch is over, comrades, we must make our way back.

(MANUELITA skips over to the trunk and crouches by it.)

I've decided that the girls from school are professional enough to help out with Cedar's protest.

(MANUELITA takes out the Hawaiian dancer.)

Any day now.

(MANUELITA puts the Barbie underneath her T-shirt, climbs over the trunk and makes her way to Cedar. She climbs it. She pulls the Barbie out, cautiously.

Slide: "Compartmentalized struggle."

MANUELITA talks directly to the Barbie.)

You can be my top secret right-hand woman in this compartmentalized struggle.

"Oh, good."

Your political name will be Tania. But remember. You must live in hiding and break all contact with the world as you knew it.

"Okay."

(MANUELITA kisses the Barbie and hides her in the tree. She then climbs out of the tree and lands on the floor, on her knees.)

Me and Joselito are back in the bathtub. It's around three in the morning and we've got some liquid paper that Joselito stole from his teacher's desk without anybody noticing, and now he's holding a match up to the passports while I blot out the big huge marks.

(MANUELITA mimes blowing out the match and then covers her mouth.)

We hear somebody coming out of Calladita's room. The person makes their way to the living room, where Juan of the Chickens is laughing in his sleep. Now Calladita's laughing too. Juan of the Chickens and Calladita moan and groan and sigh and talk in deep voices and we hear bodies moving and kissing sounds and rustling sheets. They're doing it! We wait until the moaning turns into loud vowel sounds and quickly climb out of the bathtub and hit the decks in our room. We both know that this is another one of our secrets and that we are blood brothers once again.

(MANUELITA stands up.

Slide: pictures of the disappeared with candles around them.)

My mom and dad look kinda skinny. It's been two weeks now of just water and they have to drag themselves to the bathroom 'cause they can't stand. Everybody's lying around and now that us kids are here they wanna know exactly what we've eaten. So I start telling them how I found twenty-five cents so I got a Revello, and everybody moans—

(MANUELITA walks over to the trunk and starts putting on a frilly nightgown and sheer housecoat over it.)

—and Joselito tells about eating the *cazuela* that Calladita and Juan of the Chickens make and everybody moans again and Juan of the Chickens tells about the fried chicken he eats and everybody moans again and he says there's no reason to moan 'cause it tastes like shit. Just then Crespa turns the TV on and there's a chicken commercial and everybody moans again.

Juan of the Chickens announces that today is a very special day 'cause us kids have prepared a play to entertain the strikers and get their minds off fucking food.

(MANUELITA stands on the trunk. Fairy tale music accompanies the following line.)

This play is called *Cinderella.*

(MANUELITA lies back on the trunk, miming holding a cigarette.)

"Oh, Cinderella, have you dusted the picture of the Virgin that's hanging up over my bed yet?"

(MANUELITA gets up from the trunk and does two spins.)

"No, stepmother, I've just finished dusting the legs of your queen-size bed."

(MANUELITA walks around, miming smoking.)

"Well, don't just stand there like a *rota* and remember to starch the bow on my poodle's head, poor thing."

(MANUELITA does two spins.)

"I've got Pictua right here, stepmother. I'll also give her a bath in salts too, just like you asked."

(MANUELITA walks, smoking.)

"The ball is going to be magnificent, girls. Marble floors and crystal chandeliers like you've never seen ..."

(MANUELITA leans on the desk and has a huge coughing fit. She horks.)

"And royalty: dukes, counts, princes: choose well, girls, choose well."

(MANUELITA puts a black sock on each hand and crouches behind the desk, doing puppets.)

"Of course, mother."

"We would never disappoint you."

(*MANUELITA spins.*)

"May I go to the ball too, stepmother?"

(*MANUELITA walks, smoking.*)

"Hee-hee. Did you hear that, girls? This *rota piojosa* wants to go to the ball. Once you've washed and waxed all the floors, plucked the chickens, taken care of all the mouse traps, finished embroidering that tablecloth, milked the cows and re-planted the orchard maybe I'll let you go to the ball, silly. Hee, hee."

(*MANUELITA has a huge coughing fit and horks. She waves.*)

"Bye-bye! Have a nice time at the ball!"

(*MANUELITA starts crying and collapses onto the floor as she cleans it with her nightgown.*

We hear fairy godmother music. MANUELITA stands up, very erect.)

"Don't cry, little one. You don't need to take this exploitation from the bourgeoisie. Come join me in the struggle for the proletariat and fight for a more just society, comrade."

(*MANUELITA goes back to the floor.*)

"But, who are you?"

(*MANUELITA stands up again, holding out the housecoat as if it were a cape.*)

"I am Tania, the guerilla. And that over there is Ché."

(*MANUELITA takes two steps to the side and holds up her left fist.*)

"Hasta la victoria siepre."

(*MANUELITA spins.*)

"Nice to meet you."

(*MANUELITA holds her cape out.*)

"Come with us. We're up there, in the mountains. And bring that chicken while you're at it. We're starving."

(*MANUELITA spins.*)

"But what about my stepmother?"

(*MANUELITA holds her cape out.*)

"Fuck her."

("Trabajdores Al Poder" by Karaxu begins to play as MANUELITA takes her costume off and bows. She puts it in the trunk and takes out her "Keep Your Dirty Hands Off Cedar" sign.)

"Trabajadores trampolé! Trabajadores trampolé!"

(MANUELITA goes up her tree.)

Everybody's here. Joselito and all the other kids and Lassie and the other girls from school.

(MANUELITA puts the sign around her neck.)

Everybody from the neighbourhood is coming around to see what we're doing and Lassie is explaining about how poor Cedar is going to be chopped down to make a house. They all have petitions and people are signing them. I see Bill. He's coming with the people from the TV! Everybody's jumping up and down with excitement and Lassie keeps yelling, "Look, Manolita! Look! The TV's here!"

I wanna climb down from my tree but Joselito points out that the protest will be stronger if I just stay up her with my sign. The TV people are filming all of us and Bill is talking to them. Now they're interviewing Joselito and Lassie, who are my spokespeople, and the cameraman is filming me!

(MANUELITA waves at the TV, with a big smile on her face. She then regains her composure and becomes very serious, pointing to her sign. She holds up her left fist.)

More and more people from the neighbourhood are coming and the tractor people are just getting back from their lunch break. They look kind of shocked.

"Get your dirty hands off Cedar! Don't touch Cedar!"

(Slide: two little Chilean girls at school. This later dissolves into a slide of Valparaíso.

MANUELITA starts to read a postcard. The "Letter" song plays throughout.)

Queridísima Manuela:

Como lo estas pasando en Canadá? Debe Haber mucha nieve y todo debe ser muy blanco. I miss you. At school, there's nobody there to sing the Chilean national anthem with me any more, there's nobody to sit beside and giggle at Senorita Negretti's moustache with. Your grandma is really sad that you're gone. She says she never thought it would be so long.

I still play with the doll you left for me to take care of till you came back, and every day I wear that necklace that we made out of buttons and I dream about you every night. Do you like the postcard? See how Valparaíso is the same as when you left?

Hugs and kisses,

Gabriela.

P.S. Doña Olvido from the vegetable store says hi and so does Don Pablo from the bakery.

(MANUELITA shows the postcard to her Barbie.)

I wish she'd send me a picture of herself, Tania. I barely remember what she looks like.

("El Pueblo Unido Jamás Será Vencido" by Inti-Illimani begins to play. MANUELITA hears it and climbs down from Cedar. She stands up stage right and ends up sitting on the trunk.

Slide: the Mothers of the Disappeared protesting in Chile.)

The hunger strike is finally over and everybody's here, celebrating. Even the doctor that took care of everybody. He's Palestinian and my mom explained that he went to check the strikers for free, 'cause he and his Palestinian friends are in solidarity with us. All the adults are hugging and kissing me and Joselito and the other kids 'cause they saw us on TV. My mom and dad are real proud of me. I can tell from the way they're talking about me to the other adults. The doctor's making sure nobody pigs out, but Pelao and Gordo have already made themselves an eighteen-egg omelette and are eating it straight out of the pan. My mom and dad look happy 'cause they say the hunger strike was a success. But I don't really get it 'cause the disappeared are still disappeared, but they explained this thing to me about raising awareness or something like that. Some of the adults are worried 'cause they lost their jobs while they were on strike, but everybody's still eating and drinking and telling jokes when we get a call from Chile. My mom answers and everybody gathers around.

(MANUELITA stands up. The sound of a dial tone starts and gets louder and louder throughout the next section.)

My mom gets less and less happy. Her mouth drops open and she drops the phone. My dad picks it up and he just shakes his head as he listens and says, "Ayayay." Finally he hangs up.

My grandmother is dead.

(MANUELITA runs to Cedar and climbs it.

Slide: Grandmother; it dissolves into Chilean women gathered in protest in Chile.)

My mom phoned the Chilean consul and begged him to give her a twenty-four permit to go to Valparaíso to bury my grandmother. The consul said, "Over my dead body you fucking Communist bitch." I just sit here. Keeping Cedar company. My parents and the other adults always say we kids don't remember anything, but right now I'm on the train to Santiago with my grandmother and we're buying *churros* at the Cerro Santa Lucía ... *Caballito blanco llévame de aquí, llévame a mi pueblo donde yo nací, tengo tengo tengo tú no tienes nada ...*

(MANUELITA slowly pulls the blonde wig off and fixes her hair. She looks at her hand holding the wig in her lap and hides her hand behind her back, covering the white nail polish.)

When my mother begged the consul to go and bury her mother, I showed her the passports, I told her that I'd gotten rid of the marks so she could go, but she just cried harder and said, "You poor thing," so I hugged her.

(MANUELITA looks straight ahead. She climbs down from the tree and starts tying herself to Cedar with a rope.)

Calladita told me about the Mothers and Wives of the Disappeared chaining themselves to the Presidential Palace in Chile.

(MANUELITA finishes tying herself and then puts her sign on.)

The tractors are coming. Straight for Cedar.

(MANUELITA stares straight ahead, ready. The lights go black and a single headlight shines onto her face from down stage left.

"Al Final de Este Viaje en la Vida" by Isabel Parra begins to play. The song plays in its entirety, through the walkout.

The end.)

THE FACE IS THE PLACE

BY
BETH GOOBIE

To the students of
Guelph Collegiate Vocational Institute
with thanks to the original cast and crew,
and Brian Conway

The Face is the Place was commissioned by Guelph Collegiate Vocational Institute and first performed at GCVI in 1998, with the following cast and crew:

HILARY	Sarah Dryden
STELLA	Leigh-Anne Stafford
PENNY	Carla Henderson
JANEY	Kelly Vrooman
MONICA	Ingrid Obls
RITA	Olivia MacLeod
KEVIN	Andrew Hood
LEONA	Tashlin Lakhani
DARYL	Trevor Crowe

Directed by Brian Conway
Music composed by Tim Kramer
Stage Manager: Heather Pickup
Lighting by Phil Glazebrook
Sound by Ross Ledingham
Set construction by D. Johnson
Props by Jennifer Soule
Costumes by Melissa Nolan

Special thanks to
Cathy Beamish, Alec George,
Elaine McCarron, and Al Morrison

Note

Some characters' names have changed since the original production. The character Penny is now DI; Monica is now MARION; Rita is now RITZ; and Leona is now NANNETTE. All other characters retain their original names.

Characters

HILARY: Teenager; former leader of the Faces.

STELLA: Teenager; leader of the Faces.

JANEY: Teenager; a new recruit to the Faces.

DI: Teenager; a member of the Faces.

MARION: Teenager.

RITZ: Teenager; a member of the Faces.

KEVIN: Teenager; Hilary's twin.

NANNETTE: Teenager.

DARYL: Teenager; Stella's boyfriend and Hilary's former boyfriend.

Setting

A high school, and homes in
the surrounding neighbourhood.
The present.

Scene One

HILARY: *(Playing with a knife as she speaks.)* The Face is the place you live or die. Where you make it or you lose it. Where you smile or scream. It's home or hell, and you live with what you're born with every minute of every day. So you practice the Face, work it out in the mirror, check out the angles, arrange and rearrange the details. Try out all the colours. The Face is your trophy, what you win for all those hours of practice with the enemy mirror. And when you're finished pleasing the enemy, you head out onto the front lines. Parties, school. Other faces watching your face, what you do with it, how you pull it off, how you laugh when blood's coming at you, your own blood rising inside you like a scream. Are you in control? Is your face a magnet pulling other faces toward you or is it an opposing force, pushing them away? Sure, there's boobs and ass, legs and hair. Guys look at those too, you've got to keep them in gear. But the Face is the place. Without the Face you are nothing, hear me? Nothing. The Face is your honour. You keep it clean. The Face is the place you live or die. Live or die.

Scene Two

(A girls' washroom in a high school. There are three cubicles. On one door, a sign reads: "Temporarily out of order." STELLA, JANEY, and DI hang around the mirror, putting on make-up.)

STELLA: There is a death zit on my forehead!

JANEY: Don't pop it. Your pores will get bigger.

STELLA: I can't get a zit. I'm going out with Daryl tonight. He does not appreciate zits.

DI: *(Checking out STELLA's zit.)* This is not your average pustule, Stella. This is an enormous pustule.

JANEY: Must be stress. This school is a war zone.

STELLA: This school is a zit zone. Daryl does not appreciate zits.

(The door to the bathroom opens. It remains open a moment, then swings closed. No one enters.)

JANEY: Maybe if you pop it quick and put Clearisil on it.

STELLA: Then bubbles of pus keep coming out. I can't walk around with bubbles of pus coming out of my face.

(The bathroom door opens again. Pause, then it closes.)

That door is getting on my nerves. It's only allowed to open when I say so. Open Sesame. Close Sesame. Open Sesame.

(The door opens and MARION walks in. She sees the Faces and turns quickly to leave. DI blocks her exit.)

You're here to use the facilities? Feel free.

(MARION's shoulders slump. Without a word she enters a cubicle.)

JANEY: No teenager should have to walk around with a zit on her face. I'm going into medical research to discover the cure for zits.

STELLA: What'll they call you? Madame Pustule, like Madame Curie?

(MARION emerges. Grimly she washes and dries her hands. The Faces watch silently. Finished, MARION turns and waits.)

This can happens to be the private property of the Faces.

MARION: It's a public—

(DI moves toward her. MARION backs into the wall and DI closes in.)

STELLA: As I was saying, this can is ours. No one pees in our toilets without permission. Did you ask permission?

MARION: You said feel free.

STELLA: But did you ask permission?

MARION: I thought you ran the west side washroom. I thought this one was unclaimed.

STELLA: That was last week.

MARION: It's not fair.

(DI slides her finger across her own left cheek.)

Uh, I'm not arguing. What d'you want?

STELLA: You tell her, Janey.

JANEY: Five bucks.

MARION: Five bucks to pee?

DI: Inflation.

MARION: I've only got two on me.

(She digs in her pocket and hands a lot of change to DI. DI hands it to STELLA who counts it out on the counter.)

STELLA: Two dollars and five cents. You owe us three bucks. Plus interest. Interest is five bucks an hour.

MARION: What?

STELLA: We'll need a deposit. See what she's got, Di.

DI: Necklace. How much is it worth?

MARION: Not much.

JANEY: She's lying. That pearl is real.

(She removes it from MARION's neck and hands it to STELLA.)

STELLA: Five bucks an hour plus three bucks remainder. If you want this back.

MARION: It was my grandmother's.

STELLA: I forgot to charge you for using our sinks. Maybe extra for lying about this valuable heirloom.

(MARION flees. As she goes out the door, RITZ comes in.)

RITZ: Victim number one?

STELLA: Four. Works better switching cans every few days.

(RITZ sits on the counter opposite STELLA and looks in the mirror.)

RITZ: Hello Gorgeous. Have a nice day.

(She starts examining her face.)

STELLA: So what'd you find out, Ritz?

RITZ: I don't think it's true. Just a story going around.

STELLA: If it is true, if she even looked at my Daryl, I'll cut her.

JANEY: I'm sure she didn't, Stella. She knows Daryl's yours.

STELLA: You've got to learn, Janey. Any girl tries to steal your guy, you scar her face.

RITZ: She's still going with Andrew. I saw them in the back seat of his car. All over each other.

STELLA: So, was Daryl around?

RITZ: Doesn't he have basketball practice at lunch? He wasn't bouncing his ball around her, if that's what you mean. Hey d'you think my nose looks broken? There's a bump in the middle of it. I inherited it from my mother. Did you know genes cause noses? This nose is our family tree.

DI: Looks like a redwood.

RITZ: Maybe I should get surgery. I'm tired of sitting all day in class, trying to figure out how to sit so no one can see my profile. I'm all stressed out.

DI: Your nose would stress me out.

JANEY: I like your nose, Ritz. It blends in real well with the rest of your face.

DI: Sometimes it catches the light at odd angles, though. You can get a weird glare coming off that bump.

(STELLA gives DI a grin. RITZ catches it.)

RITZ: *(Casually.)* I heard something today.

STELLA: About my Daryl?

RITZ: About Hilary.

(There is a sudden pause.)

STELLA: *(Instinctively touching her left cheek.)* Oh yeah.

JANEY: Hilary?

RITZ: I heard she's coming back.

DI: No way.

JANEY: Are you serious?

STELLA: She wouldn't show her face in this place. I heard she scratched the other half up bad herself.

RITZ: She did. I saw a picture of her. My brother knows her neighbour. They jumped her in her back yard, held her down and took a picture.

JANEY: What's she look like?

RITZ: Bad. Frankenstein.

(The door opens. MARION bursts in and places three dollars on the counter.)

MARION: There. Now you have the whole five dollars. Can I have my necklace, please?

STELLA: I think I'll keep the family heirloom. Payment for using my sink.

MARION: But you said—

(STELLA remains apart, watching, as the rest of the Faces close in around MARION.)

DI: *(Touching MARION's left cheek.)* You want to be ugly?

RITZ: *(Touching MARION's left cheek.)* You want to be scarred?

MARION: No.

JANEY: *(Touching MARION's left cheek.)* You want to be clean, untouched.

> *(The Faces step back and STELLA rushes MARION and shoves her.)*

STELLA: Get out of my office or your face is the place.

> *(STELLA steps back and MARION slips out without a word.)*

I'm tired of this can. It has no ambience. I like the west side better. You got that picture on you, Ritz?

RITZ: They wouldn't give it to me.

STELLA: She wouldn't come back. There's no life after death, y'know.

> *(She fakes clawing her own face and grins. The others smile in agreement.)*

Her face died and now her life is over.

> *(The Faces exit.)*

Scene Three

(DI stands alone on stage.)

DI: We're the Keepers of the Face. We call ourselves the Faces, we're the Keepers of the Face. The Face. All faces belong to the Face. No matter which girl's wearing it, every face belongs to the Face. The Face rules. If a girl follows the Code, her face stays clean. If she breaks the Code, we claim her skin. The Face is your beauty, it's what people look at to decide if you're in or out. I'd kill to protect my face. Any girl tried to steal my beauty, I'd make her remember what she did every time she looked in a mirror. I'm always ready, I know where my razors are, where I keep them hidden. Hilary wasn't ready. She passed out at a party and someone got to her. No one was around, no one saw who did it. Hilary was the toughest but she wasn't ready. Now she's dead in the mirror, no one will look at her, her future's her past. The Face is the place. The Face is the place.

> *(DI exits.)*

Scene Four

(Hilary's bedroom. HILARY sits on her bed, playing solitaire. A guitar lies nearby. Her twin brother KEVIN enters and flops down beside her, messing up the cards.)

HILARY: Kevin, I was winning.

KEVIN: No one wins at solitaire.

HILARY: I got really good at it in that place. Us psychos are experts at solitaire.

KEVIN: Well, now you're out of there. You're here. And you're not psycho.

(*He starts collecting and stacking the cards. He looks at the guitar.*)

You singing again?

HILARY: No.

KEVIN: You want to go for a walk?

HILARY: No.

KEVIN: Just out to the back yard?

HILARY: No.

KEVIN: I'll be with you. It won't happen with me there.

HILARY: No.

KEVIN: Hil, you've got to go out sometime. You're starting school Monday.

HILARY: I know. (*She gets up and paces.*) It's too bright out.

KEVIN: They keep the lights on at school.

HILARY: I'm not stupid.

KEVIN: Why don't you go to Wilson High like Mom suggested. Different school, nobody knows you.

HILARY: They will soon. One look at my ... (*Pause.*) I need to come back here. Things to finish. How's Daryl?

KEVIN: Don't waste your time on that creep. He didn't call once while you were in treatment.

HILARY: "In treatment." How sweet of you.

KEVIN: Well, you were in treatment. Not a nut house.

HILARY: It was a locked ward.

KEVIN: You needed it.

HILARY: Oooo. Little brother changed while I was gone.

KEVIN: I'm not little. I'm your twin. I'm not saying you need that place now. You're stronger, I can tell.

HILARY: Thank you, Doctor Kevin. When did you get your degree?

KEVIN: Growing up with you.

HILARY: He's with Stella, isn't he?

KEVIN: Stella did it to you, y'know.

HILARY: How would you know?

KEVIN: That's what the story is. She cut you so she could run the Faces and grab Daryl.

HILARY: Stella wouldn't do that to me. We're the Faces, we're together.

KEVIN: Did she call you? Did she call once while you were in there? Did any of them call you?

HILARY: Her face is clean.

KEVIN: Yeah, her *face* is clean.

HILARY: The Face is the place ... Any girl scars your face, you kill her. The Face has to be clean. If she did it, if she stole my face, she has it coming and she knows it.

KEVIN: Geez, Hilary, I can't believe the way you're talking. You sound like the Terminator. Talk human, would ya? You're not killing anyone. C'mere. *(He pats the edge of the bed.)* C'mere and sit down.

> *(HILARY sits next to him, facing outward. He turns her so they sit facing. HILARY looks down.)*

Y'know how we're twins, and we're supposed to have this special connection?

> *(HILARY looks at him as if he's crazy.)*

I know, the impossible dream. I'm a nerd and you're real pop. You look like Mom and I look like the alien that got at her one night in her sleep, and we came out together. And ... I've always been scared of you.

HILARY: No.

KEVIN: C'mon, Hil—you're the Face, you're the toughest, so sure you can have the Cheerios first and the last of the cherry jam too, if you want. And the channel changer because no way I'm going to argue with you and your blades, wherever you've got them stashed.

HILARY: I'm not carrying any now.

KEVIN: Now I'm not scared.

> *(He reaches a hand to her left cheek. HILARY flinches and draws back, then lets him trace the knife scar and the finger scratch scars on her right cheek.)*

I felt it when she cut you, Hil.

HILARY: What?

KEVIN: I was in my room, working on Algebra, and I felt a burning pain all through my left cheek. Not just a slash, it went jagged across my face like a lightning bolt, like she cut you so no surgeon could make you look good again.

HILARY: A party with my friends.

KEVIN: When you scratched your other cheek, I felt that too.

HILARY: When I did that, when I scratched my face, I didn't feel it. I was looking in the mirror and I watched it happen. I saw the blood come, but I didn't feel it.

KEVIN: So I know some things about you, some things you don't know. I know how you *feel*. You don't know how you feel, all you know is the Face. The Face is the place but you haven't got any feelings. You've been sending them to me, Hil. You've been sending me your feelings. Well now I'm giving them back to you. The Face isn't the place, Hil. It never was.

(HILARY stiffens and looks off.)

Hil. Hil. Look at me, please. *(He traces her left cheek.)* Just look at me.

(After a long moment, HILARY's eyes meet KEVIN's. They continue to look in each other's eyes as KEVIN speaks.)

This is what I know. I know you're afraid of eyes—the way they look at you, the way they size you up, add you up like a popularity equation. Face plus boobs plus ass equals ... what? What does it equal? Now it doesn't matter, because your face got cut.

HILARY: I'm dead in the mirror. The Face is dead.

KEVIN: I love this face, Hil. I'm not afraid of it anymore. When you had the other face, I used to get dreams where you came at me screaming with razors on your fingertips. Now that face is gone. You're my sister. You're human. I love this face. Keep looking at me Hil, keep looking at me. Just keep looking in my eyes, because eyes are going to be looking at you, and you need to be able to look back. This is practice. We'll practice all weekend. All weekend I'm going to be looking in your eyes, and you're going to look at me, and no one's going to be afraid.

(Pause, the two of them look at each other.)

HILARY: Who are you, Kevin?

KEVIN: You're going to find out. *(He takes HILARY's hand and squeezes it.)* C'mon, let's go for a walk.

(They exit.)

Scene Five

(School hallway. NANNETTE and MARION enter, talking. They open their lockers, which are situated on opposite walls, continuing their conversation.)

NANNETTE: It is getting harder and harder to take a decent pee in this school. I mean, how long can you hold it? It's not like you can decide mind over matter and the stuff stops coming out. It's a basic function.

MARION: They're playing Musical Washrooms now. Nowhere is safe.

NANNETTE: Friday they got me again—third time last week. I paid my tax and they still wouldn't let me use the toilet. They said I smelled bad and they didn't want me to stink up the place. I do not smell bad.

MARION: Even the teachers are scared of the Faces.

NANNETTE: Teachers have their own cans. They're safe. Y'know what really bugs me? This school is being run by a bunch of girls with single-digit IQs.

(She frowns thoughtfully, then yells and attempts a round-house kick. She wobbles and stumbles. A pause, then she tries again. She stops and grins.)

Hey, this is cool.

(She tries a karate chop. Suddenly she stops and slumps.)

What's this going to do against a bunch of blades?

MARION: We're all doomed.

(DARYL enters and walks up to MARION.)

DARYL: Hey, Marion.

MARION: *(Nervously.)* Oh, hi Daryl.

DARYL: So, how's it going?

MARION: All right, I guess. You know Monday mornings.

(DARYL removes her necklace from his jacket pocket and holds it out to her.)

DARYL: I've got something for you.

MARION: *(Taking it.)* How did you get this?

DARYL: She told me she took it from you. She was spaced, so she didn't notice when I took it off her neck. I thought you'd want it back.

MARION: Thanks.

(She puts it on and tucks it under her shirt so no one can see it.)

DARYL: So, how was your weekend?

MARION: The usual.

DARYL: So, you seeing anyone?

(MARION doesn't answer.)

You busy on Friday night?

MARION: Aren't you seeing Stella?

DARYL: She doesn't own me. Besides … *(He reaches out and touches her cheek.)* I like your face.

MARION: *(Stepping back as if burnt.)* She'll cut me.

DARYL: I won't let her.

MARION: You planning on coming into the can with me?

DARYL: Sure.

(The Faces walk into the hallway. STELLA sees DARYL and MARION and freezes.)

RITZ: Would you look at this.

(MARION sees the Faces and gasps. DARYL turns toward them.)

DARYL: Stella.

(He walks to STELLA, puts his arm around her, and leans her against the wall.)

JANEY: *(To MARION.)* Who d'you think you're talking to?

DI: *(To MARION.)* Your face is ours, bitch.

STELLA: *(To DARYL.)* You didn't call me yesterday.

DARYL: I didn't wake up 'til two. You wore me out.

STELLA: Not last night either.

RITZ: *(To DI and JANEY.)* C'mon, let's check out this face close up.

STELLA: *(To DARYL.)* Why were you talking to her?

DARYL: I was waiting for you and she just showed up.

(RITZ, JANEY, and DI move in on MARION. MARION starts grabbing things from her locker.)

DI: Think you're going somewhere?

JANEY: Yeah, think you're going somewhere?

STELLA: *(To DARYL.)* My necklace is missing.

DARYL: Must have fallen off when we got going.

(STELLA giggles.)

RITZ: *(Taking hold of MARION's arm.)* Gotcha.

NANNETTE: Um. Excuse me? Leave her alone.

(The Faces notice NANNETTE.)

RITZ: Hey, it's the face with the odour problem.

(RITZ drops MARION's arm. The Faces focus on NANNETTE.)

Sewer Face, you're ugly.

DI: Your face needs to be recycled.

JANEY: Yeah, recycled. And you owe us.

NANNETTE: I paid you.

RITZ: So what you keep in your locker, Sewer Face?

NANNETTE: *(Taking a deep breath.)* You are trespassing in my personal contact zone.

DI: What did you say?

(HILARY and KEVIN enter and stand at the end of the hall.)

RITZ: Would you look at that.

(The others turn and stare. DARYL keeps his arm around STELLA. DI whistles. Everyone parts to leave an empty path down the middle of the hall. There is absolute silence. HILARY takes one step forward, trying to meet their eyes. As she looks at each person, their eyes shift away. Everyone stares at HILARY as long as she isn't looking at them, but no one will meet her eyes. HILARY takes another step, then seems to falter. KEVIN takes her hand. Together they walk slowly down the hall between the staring students, then exit off stage.)

DARYL: Is she a mess.

STELLA: The afterlife.

RITZ: Told ya. Frankenstein.

JANEY: Her face is meat.

DI: Raw.

DARYL: Wonder what she turns into after midnight, eh?

STELLA: You don't need her, you've got me.

(STELLA and DARYL kiss and walk off stage.)

RITZ: *(To MARION.)* You're on our time now.

DI: *(To MARION.)* When we decide. *(To NANNETTE.)* Watch it, Sewer Face.

JANEY: Yeah, watch it.

(RITZ, DI, and JANEY exit. MARION stands staring after them.)

NANNETTE: *(To their disappearing backs.)* Don't take yourselves so personally. *(She turns to MARION.)* You all right?

MARION: I don't know.

NANNETTE: I'd like to shellac their faces.

(MARION and NANNETTE exit.)

Scene Six

(The girls' washroom. JANEY stands alone, holding an orange.)

JANEY: Sometimes I get this feeling there's something sliding down my face. I touch my face and it's slippery. I look at my fingers and they're covered in blood. Everywhere I touch my face, little tiny cuts open under my fingers. I'm cutting my face just by touching it. I'm awake. I'm not dreaming. Then it passes. I look in the mirror and the Face is clean. But I'm not there. I can see the Face, untouched, the way it's supposed to be, but I'm not in the Face. I'm in a second face. The second face is in behind the Face. The second face is me. It has cuts all over it and they're bleeding. Sometimes my two faces look at each other. The clean face starts laughing at the bleeding face. It's like they go together. You can't have the clean untouched face without the other face bleeding inside it. Two-faced. What I want to know is how do I make the bleeding stop? How do I make it stop?

(JANEY starts to peel the orange, then stops and stands staring at the mirror. DI enters.)

DI: Stella late again?

JANEY: Di, you ever, like, see other dimensions?

DI: Huh?

JANEY: There's like this horror movie, but it's in my face. How do I make it go away?

DI: Blink real fast. Shake your head like this.

(STELLA and RITZ enter.)

STELLA: I'm calling this meeting of the Faces to order.

JANEY: *(Nervously.)* Did you know that Vasco de Gama figured out the world was round while he was peeling an orange?

RITZ: Guess we're lucky he wasn't peeling a banana.

STELLA: Shut up about fruit. We're here to discuss Janey's initiation assignment.

(DI takes the orange from JANEY, breaks it into pieces, and hands some to STELLA and RITZ. They eat the orange as the scene progresses.)

STELLA: You know the girl who's insulted the honour of the Faces.

JANEY: Marion Sainsbury.

STELLA: She's trying to steal one of our guys. Your initiation assignment is to avenge our honour.

JANEY: How?

STELLA: Cut Marion Sainsbury's left cheek.

JANEY: I have to cut her face? I've never cut a face before.

DI: You're a fighter, Janey. I've seen you fight.

JANEY: Cut a face? I don't think I—

RITZ: You've got to enforce the Code. You're one of the Faces.

STELLA: Or maybe you don't want to be? You're in or you're out, Janey. You know what happens if you break the Code.

(JANEY gasps and touches her own left cheek.)

You think about it. Pick a time and place and we'll be there to back you up. Since it's your first time. It'll be your true initiation.

RITZ: We're the Keepers of the Face, Janey.

JANEY: Keepers of the Face.

STELLA: Well, Daryl's waiting for me. Gotta run. Coming, Ritz?

RITZ: Yeah.

(STELLA and RITZ exit. DI and JANEY stand silently.)

JANEY: Will this make it stop, Di? If I cut her face, if I make her face bleed, will my face stop bleeding?

DI: What are you talking about? Your face isn't bleeding. It's just a trick your mind's playing on you, trying to get you to be weak. This will make you tough. When you're tough, you don't care about blood.

(DI and JANEY exit.)

Scene Seven

(School hallway. HILARY enters and stands at her locker. She opens it, then stands staring vaguely. She hums part of a song that's developing in her head.)

HILARY: *(Singing softly.)*
It's dark now, I'm feeling my way.

It's dark now, it's dark now, I'm feeling my way.
I've turned out the lights to meet this stranger ...

(She looks around, sees no one, and pulls out a pocket mirror. Briefly she looks at the knife scar, then shoves the mirror back into her pocket. MARION enters, sees HILARY, and stops. MARION observes HILARY in runaway glances. HILARY ignores her.)

MARION: Excuse me.

(HILARY ignores her.)

Could I ... could I talk to you? Just for a second?

HILARY: What for?

MARION: I'm not sure.

HILARY: Second's up.

MARION: I, uh ... Oh, never mind.

(MARION turns to leave.)

HILARY: You scared of me?

MARION: Do you want me to be?

HILARY: Yeah.

MARION: Why?

HILARY: Hey, I just got out of a psych ward. I'm not answering any more questions.

(A pause. The two girls watch each other.)

MARION: Look, I know I'm not like you, we're different—

HILARY: No kidding.

MARION: They're after me.

HILARY: So you're afraid you'll end up like me.

MARION: How do I stop it?

HILARY: You're asking me?

MARION: How does it feel?

HILARY: Looking like this? More than I've ever felt. More than I knew I could feel. It's all here now. *(She gestures at her face.)* Right here.

MARION: Can't you get surgery?

HILARY: The skin has to heal. You've got to live with it until the skin's ready.

MARION: But they can fix it. Take it away.

HILARY: No one can take this away.

MARION: I feel like it's already happened. Like the scars are already under my face, waiting to happen. *They* just have to pick the time and place.

HILARY: That's right.

> *(She pulls out a switchblade and flicks it open.)*

You want lessons?

> *(She holds it out to MARION, who stares at it, stunned.)*

Here, it's yours. Practice on tomatoes first.

MARION: Is that what they used on you?

HILARY: I was passed out. I woke up tasting my own blood. I thought I was dreaming. What are they after you for?

MARION: Daryl Zawalski talked to me.

HILARY: Daryl?

MARION: Stella saw him talking to me.

HILARY: He ask you out?

MARION: Yeah.

> *(HILARY's face grows hostile.)*

> *(Quickly.)* But I said no.

> *(HILARY grabs MARION's hair, pulls her head back, and holds the blade to her left cheek. MARION drops her books.)*

HILARY: Your name's Marion, right?

MARION: Yes.

HILARY: Well, Marion, the Faces go for the left cheek. It's their trademark. It'll happen something like this. If I was still one of them, it'd be over by now, you got it?

MARION: Yes.

HILARY: *(Releasing her.)* What you need is a little friend, so I'm giving you this.

> *(She closes the switchblade and places it in MARION's hand.)*

So long, Marion.

> *(She walks away.)*

MARION: But …

HILARY: *(Whirling suddenly.)* You didn't come to talk to a person, you came to talk to the Face. Well, the Face has spoken.

> *(She exits. MARION stares after HILARY, then at the switchblade. She picks up her books and exits.)*

Scene Eight

(RITZ stands alone on stage.)

RITZ: When you cut, there's a texture to it. If you're really tuned, you can feel the change between air and skin. And cutting deeper. There's blood, this isn't Biology class, her face isn't waiting for you pickled and smiling, saying, "Cut here for an A-plus." This is *alive*, moving and screaming. Fear. It's her face or yours, and everything comes down to the edge of your blade. Your whole life rides on the edge of your blade because if she gets you, you're over. Dead in the face. You can't be a Maybe Girl—maybe I will, maybe I won't. Maybe Girls get nowhere in life. Their whole life's a maybe, just like their faces. The Faces—we know who we are. We're committed. You look in my face and you know who I am. See any maybes here? Hilary allowed one maybe. The Face is the place. The Face is the place.

Scene Nine

(STELLA enters a school washroom and begins to preen in the mirror. HILARY enters. They freeze and stare at each other. STELLA's hand slides to her pocket.)

STELLA: So, uh, how are you, Hil? You're lookin' good.

HILARY: The Face is the place, Stella.

(Long pause as they watch each other.)

Did you do it?

STELLA: C'mon, the Faces stick together.

HILARY: Not any more.

STELLA: You got scarred. You know the Code.

HILARY: Yeah, I know the Code. You know the Code too.

STELLA: So you figure out who did it and you take revenge. The Faces will back you. Just let us know when and where.

HILARY: Because of the Code.

STELLA: We know the Code.

HILARY: But does the Code know me?

STELLA: I don't know what you're talking about.

(STELLA pushes past HILARY and exits. HILARY stands facing the door.)

HILARY: Stella.

(HILARY exits.)

Scene Ten

(A party at Stella's house. The Faces and DARYL are present. STELLA is very drunk and sits snuggled into DARYL.)

DI: She wasn't a virgin. She was never a virgin.

JANEY: Virgin is a state of mind.

STELLA: I say she asked for it. What d'you think, Daryl?

DARYL: You're right.

STELLA: Right again. *(She takes a drink.)* I love being right. I am always right. Even when I am wrong, I am right. Even when I am evil, I am right. I could do anything I wanted, and I'd get away with it, and I'd still be right. I got the guy I wanted, didn't I? Best, most wonderful guy in the world and you're mine, aren't you, Daryl?

DARYL: You're loaded, Stella.

STELLA: But I'm right, aren't I?

DARYL: You're my girl, Stella.

STELLA: Right is a state of mind and I've got it.

RITZ: You've sure got something.

JANEY: Let's go out. I'm hungry. Why don't we get a burger?

RITZ: So, how did you get away with it, Stella?

STELLA: Get away with what?

RITZ: You know what I'm talking about.

(STELLA giggles. Another pause.)

JANEY: I'm really starved. Let's go out.

STELLA: Always keep your eyes open. And if you take a nappy with your friends, keep your left cheek to the ground. *(Giggles.)* Right Daryl? Right?

DARYL: *(Glancing at RITZ.)* Right. You are so right.

JANEY: I got another assignment in Geography today. More rocks. Who cares about the Canadian Shield? It's just all rocks.

DI: Shut up, Janey.

JANEY: The Canadian Shield is so big it takes up half of Canada. The Canadian Shield is boring. Canada is boring. Canada needs a few volcanic eruptions. Then geography would be more interesting. I think they should happen in Saskatchewan, maybe once a month—

(DI claps her hand over JANEY's mouth. Everyone sits waiting.)

STELLA: Give me another beer.

DARYL: Give the girl another beer, Ritz.

RITZ: Here's your beer, Stella. Drink up.

(STELLA drinks. DARYL strokes her arm and hair. No one speaks. STELLA laughs loudly.)

STELLA: She was so stupid. Thought she had the whole world wrapped around her little finger. You remember how she was. Hilary could do no wrong. Everything she did was right. Right?

DARYL: Right.

STELLA: She pissed me off. So sure of herself. You didn't really like her, Daryl. You really liked me but Hilary was always in the way. You knew if you asked me out, Hilary would come after me and you wouldn't do that to me, you know what my face means to me, don't you, Daryl?

(DARYL touches STELLA's cheek but doesn't say anything.)

It was all up to me. I had to solve the problem because I was the only one who could. Juliet and Romeo, y'know. I did it for love.

(She gets to her knees and reenacts the scene.)

So she's passed out on the rec room floor. Everyone else is up-stairs watching TV. She's completely out. I can't believe it. I can do anything I want. Anything I've dreamed of doing.

I take my time. I give her chances. "Wakee wakee, Hilary, the monster's going to get you." She doesn't wake up. I poke her in the arm. She doesn't move. I poke her in the stomach. She doesn't move. I whisper in her ear, "Hilary, the monster's coming to get you." She doesn't move. I yell, "Hey, Hilary!" I even shake her so hard her head flops around. "Wake up, you're going to lose your face." Nothing. So I tell her, "All right Hilary, I gave you chances. A million and one chances. I was more generous than anyone else would be. You can understand that, can't you? This is about love. This is for Daryl because I love him more than you do, and it's my turn now."

I take out my blade. I think, "Your parents are lawyers, they've got money, this has to be messy or they'll smooth it over. Like it never happened. And you're so good with the Face, Hilary, you'll pull it off. You'll wear your new face like it was clean, and every-one will forget you were touched, you were scarred. It has to be done right so it can't be fixed." I'm staring at her and this picture comes into my mind—a jagged cut, zigzag. I put one hand on her head to hold her down, but I keep her face turned up so everyone will see the scar no matter how she holds her head. I have the picture of it so clear in my mind, I think it'll be like cutting out sewing patterns in Home Ec. Just cut along the lines.

(Pause.)

I forgot about the blood. There was so much blood. How could I forget about the blood?

(Pause.)

But I kept my head straight. I didn't let blood scare me. I cut the exact pattern on her face, just the way I saw it in my head. The scar is right. I saw it on her face, and the scar is exactly like the picture in my head.

DI: Did she see you?

STELLA: She came to and grabbed her face, but she was so out of it. She passed out again, bleeding all over the floor.

RITZ: So she doesn't know it was you.

STELLA: I was kneeling right in front of her. "Sweet dreams," I told her. "Sweet dreams, Hilary." Then I went upstairs to watch TV. *(She snuggles back into DARYL.)* No one saw me. No one knows, not even you. *(She points at the Faces, each one in turn.)* Not even you. My face is clean. Hilary's is the face that got touched. I'm clean, right? The Face is the place, right?

(There is a long pause, everyone stares at STELLA.)

RITZ: The Face is the place.

DARYL: Right.

JANEY: I'm hungry.

DI: Let's go for a burger. Janey's dying here.

JANEY: Definitely dying.

(Everyone gets up. DARYL helps STELLA stand.)

STELLA: I'm right, I'm always right, what I did was right. The Face is the place. My face is clean, I'm right, aren't I right, Ritz?

RITZ: You're the toughest, Stella. The Face is yours.

(They exit.)

Scene Eleven

(The stage is completely dark. All the girls are on stage, separate from each other, isolated. Each sits in front of her bedroom mirror, holding an unlit flashlight in her hand. HILARY sits centre stage, facing the audience.)

HILARY *(Singing in the dark.)*
   It's dark now, I'm feeling my way
   I've turned out the lights to meet this stranger
   All my life, my eyes couldn't see her
   I've let the dark come, now I can feel her

   (Spoken.) You feel scary, stranger.

> *(HILARY sighs and turns on her flashlight, studying herself in her mirror. All the girls begin to turn their flashlights on and off at staggered intervals, sometimes one at a time, sometimes several. The girls preen, apply make-up, study their faces. NANNETTE is the only one who doesn't wear make-up. After studying her face, she puts on a plastic nose, glasses and mustache set and looks at herself. No words are spoken. There are sighs and soft groans. After a while, Hilary's flashlight remains on. She touches her scars, then every part of her face. The other girls turn off their flashlights and leave the stage. HILARY takes out a small sharp nail file. She runs her fingers over it and studies her face. As she raises the file, KEVIN enters her bedroom.)*

KEVIN: Hilary, no!

> *(KEVIN tackles HILARY from behind and wraps his arms around her. She drops the file but continues to hold the flashlight which remains on, the light swinging with her hand. They stand locked like this, rocking slightly until HILARY turns off the flashlight and they exit.)*

Scene Twelve

> *(School cafeteria. NANNETTE enters with a bag lunch and sits at a table. She is wearing the plastic nose, glasses and mustache set. KEVIN enters with a lunch tray and sits opposite her.)*

KEVIN: Hiding a zit?

NANNETTE: Maybe the Faces will think I'm someone else and leave me alone.

KEVIN: I could get you into the guys' can.

NANNETTE: I don't think so. Anyway, this face is better than the old one.

KEVIN: What's the matter with the real one?

NANNETTE: Eyes too small and not much colour. Nose: big and crooked. Mouth: thin and small. Many zits. A blackhead festival. A second mustache under this plastic one.

KEVIN: Oh. I never noticed.

NANNETTE: Never noticed what?

KEVIN: The blackhead festival. The mustache. Any of it.

NANNETTE: Oh. What did you notice?

KEVIN: Two eyes and a nose and a mouth. A regular face.

NANNETTE: Just a regular face, eh?

KEVIN: But it's *your* face.

NANNETTE: I guess.

KEVIN: You're not turning into another cosmetic surgery case, are you? What's the matter with a regular face?

NANNETTE: It's not good enough. There's only one kind of face that's good enough, and that one's on all the magazine covers. My face will definitely never be on a magazine.

KEVIN: Not if you're wearing a plastic nose.

NANNETTE: It's not my life goal, but just once I'd like to wake up in the morning and know my face could be on the front of a magazine. Just to know my face is good enough. Every time I see one of those goddam magazines, it's like a slap in the face. "Ugly," they're saying to me. "You're ugly." So this is my protest. *(She pokes at the plastic nose.)*

KEVIN: You're like Hilary.

NANNETTE: That's different.

KEVIN: No it isn't. You hate your face as much as she hates hers. It's like her whole life is her face. She thinks she isn't anything more than those scars on her face. But she is. My twin is a great singer. She used to write tons of songs before she joined the Faces. Then she stopped singing. She started talking stupid to fit in. I don't fit in, but so what? Who wants to be a fashion robot? So my face isn't anything to sing about. So I'm a terminal geek. I figured that out in grade seven. I had a vision. "Terminal" appeared on my forehead.

> *(His face looks spacey and vague as he remembers his vision.)*
"Terminal."

> *(He comes out of it and shrugs.)*

So now I check to make sure no boogers are erupting from my nostrils, and other than that, I never look in a mirror.

NANNETTE: So you hate your face too.

KEVIN: I don't stare at it for hours. *(In a high falsetto.)* "Dear Face, O Beloved Face, O Great and Shining Star, how are you today?"

(He returns to his normal voice.) My face is a function—it eats, it breathes, it scans for danger. A decoration it's not.

NANNETTE: Here. *(She hands him a fake nose set.)* It was a two-for-one sale. I've been looking for a partner in protest.

(He slides a candy bar across the table to her.)

KEVIN: It's a trade.

(He puts on the nose set. NANNETTE and KEVIN look at each other and giggle.)

It's hot in here.

NANNETTE: My nose keeps getting itchy. That's the worst. But I like being a protester. Want to hear my rebel yell?

KEVIN: Yup.

(NANNETTE emits a rebel yell. KEVIN emits a rebel yell. They look around the cafeteria.)

NANNETTE: No one noticed.

KEVIN: Maybe if there were twenty of us. Hey, where'd you get these?

NANNETTE: It's a couple of blocks.

KEVIN: C'mon.

(They exit.)

Scene Thirteen

(NANNETTE stands alone on stage.)

NANNETTE: It's caught on like wildfire. Almost everyone's joined the protest. Some of the teachers are even wearing them. We take them off for classes but as soon as the bell rings, on they come again. It's so great. I never knew everyone felt this way too. We're all sick and tired of being told we don't look good enough, we have to have the perfect face. *The Face.* Now everyone's equal. Everyone's themselves. Which is weird because we're all wearing a mask, but it *feels* like the opposite is true. It feels like our real faces are these plastic nose sets. When we put on the noses, we can be real. *(Pause.)* Y'know what's really weird? Now, when I look at magazine covers, the models look like aliens.

Scene Fourteen

(School hallway. HILARY enters, wearing a plastic nose set, and opens her locker. MARION enters, also wearing a plastic nose set.)

MARION: Hi.

HILARY: Hi.

> *(MARION walks past HILARY and exits. NANNETTE enters, wearing a fake nose set.)*

Hey.

NANNETTE: Yeah?

HILARY: This was your idea, wasn't it?

NANNETTE: Actually, it was your brother's.

HILARY: But he got it from you. You were protesting against the Face.

NANNETTE: Yeah, I was.

HILARY: People talk to me now.

NANNETTE: Welcome to the human face.

HILARY: Thanks.

> *(NANNETTE exits. DARYL walks on, wearing a fake nose set. He walks past HILARY, ignoring her. HILARY grabs his arm.)*

Look at me. Why won't you ever look at me?

> *(There is a pause. Finally, DARYL glances at the knife scar on HILARY's face. HILARY lets go of his arm. DARYL turns to walk away. KEVIN enters, wearing a plastic nose set.)*

KEVIN: *(Enraged.)* You microbe!!

DARYL: Huh?

HILARY: Kevin?

KEVIN: *(To DARYL.)* Take that off! You take that off!

DARYL: What's with you, man?

KEVIN: You don't know what it means. You can't wear it.

DARYL: I can wear anything I want.

KEVIN: *(Attacking DARYL, grabbing at his nose set.)* You don't have the right. Not after what you did to my sister.

HILARY: Kevin, it's all right. I'm all right.

> *(DARYL twists KEVIN's arm behind his back and holds him this way until noted.)*

Let him go, Daryl.

DARYL: Let's just get something straight, Kevin. I didn't do nothing. I wasn't the one who messed up her face.

KEVIN: You messed up her soul.

HILARY: Let him go.

DARYL: Are you crazy? He's nuts.

KEVIN: You're dating the girl who perpetrated an act of aggravated physical assault against your former girlfriend. What're you, a pervert?

DARYL: Keep it down.

KEVIN: What d'you do—dream about girls attacking each other with knives and razors just so they can touch your loathsome, perverted, twisted body?

DARYL: Would you shut up?

HILARY: Kevin, what do you want?

KEVIN: No wonder you need a plastic mask for a disguise. Your real face is evil.

DARYL: You're losing it, pal.

(HILARY removes DARYL's plastic nose set.)

HILARY: I've got it. I've got his mask, Kevin.

(DARYL releases KEVIN and shoves him.)

KEVIN: *(Taking the mask from HILARY.)* Don't you *ever* let me catch you wearing this again.

DARYL: Hey, never argue with a psycho.

(DARYL exits.)

HILARY: *(Patting KEVIN's shoulder.)* Calm down, Superman.

KEVIN: In the flesh.

(They smile at each other weakly. They exit.)

Scene Fifteen

(MARION stands alone on stage, holding a plastic nose set.)

MARION: It could happen to any one of us. At any moment. All it takes is one second. *(She touches her left cheek.)* Skin is made up of so many things you never think about. Everything that is you. The way you laugh, the way you cry, the way feelings run through you. You never think about it because then you realize you could lose it, it could be taken away. I am Hilary. I've got her face waiting inside mine. Hilary's face is waiting inside everyone's face. Hilary's face is the Face. Is that why we're wearing these masks?

Scene Sixteen

(The girls' washroom. HILARY enters, wearing a fake nose set. The sign on the cubicle door has been changed to read: "Terminally out of order." HILARY enters one of the other two cubicles. A moment later, MARION looks in, wearing a fake nose set. Seeing no one, she goes into the other empty cubicle. The Faces enter quietly, check under the cubicle doors, then position themselves, blocking the exit door, and wait. MARION comes out of the cubicle.)

STELLA: Well, look who we have here.

(MARION tries to back into the cubicle, but DI blocks it. RITZ pulls MARION into the center of the room. Pause. The Faces watch MARION.)

Still trying to steal my guy?

MARION: No.

RITZ: *(Shoving MARION.)* Thief.

MARION: He just talked to me. Once.

(STELLA steps forward and checks MARION's neck. She finds the necklace. MARION grabs at it and they struggle. DI and RITZ hold MARION while STELLA removes the necklace and puts it on.)

STELLA: How'd you get my necklace?

(MARION doesn't answer. RITZ shoves MARION.)

MARION: He gave it to me. I didn't ask him to, he just did.

STELLA: You're a slut trying to steal someone else's guy. Get her down.

(STELLA, RITZ, and DI wrestle MARION to the floor. JANEY is backed against a wall, watching. RITZ and DI hold MARION's arms. STELLA is sitting on MARION. STELLA removes the plastic nose.)

You're so ugly. No one would ever want you. Look at this face. *(She squishes MARION's nose, pulls at her lips.)* Monkey face, ape face. No wonder you wear one of those stupid masks. What d'you got to say for yourself, thief? Trying to steal my guy? Now you'll really need a mask. Janey.

(JANEY doesn't move.)

STELLA: Janey, get over here.

MARION: No.

(JANEY approaches slowly.)

STELLA: Where's your blade?

MARION: Janey, don't. Don't do it, please.

(JANEY takes out a razor.)

STELLA: I'll hold her feet so she's nice and steady for you. You don't want to take out her eye, do you, Janey?

JANEY: No.

STELLA: I'd lie real still, or you'll end up looking like Hilary. Do it like we showed you, Janey.

JANEY: All right.

MARION: Janey.

(JANEY kneels over MARION. RITZ, DI, and STELLA hold MARION's arms and feet. HILARY bursts out of her cubicle and jumps STELLA, knocking her onto the floor and holding her down. HILARY has already taken off her plastic nose set, letting it hang around her neck.)

STELLA: Get her!

(Startled, JANEY, RITZ, and DI let go of MARION, who scrambles away. DI moves toward HILARY and STELLA, but RITZ blocks her with an arm and shakes her head.)

C'mon you guys, get her off me.

(Again DI steps forward, but RITZ puts her arm out.)

MARION: Need some help?

HILARY: No. So, uh, how are you, Stell? You're lookin' good. Maybe not for long, eh?

STELLA: You wouldn't dare.

(The bathroom door opens and NANNETTE walks in, wearing a plastic nose set and carrying textbooks.)

NANNETTE: Holy shit.

(She backs out. The door closes, then opens again and NANNETTE walks back in. She peers down at STELLA.)

Holy shit.

(A black magic marker drops off her textbooks and falls onto the floor.)

HILARY: Give me that.

(MARION retrieves it and hands it to HILARY.)

Hold her arms.

(MARION and NANNETTE hold STELLA's arms.)

STELLA: What're you gonna do? I'll kill you if you scar me. I got you once and I'll—

HILARY: *(Yelling in her face.)* I know you did! *(To NANNETTE.)* This wash off?

NANNETTE: Indelible.

STELLA: Hey, what're you doing? Don't you touch my face. We're the Faces, we'll come after you.

HILARY: Relax, it'll wear off.

> *(She draws a replica of her own scar on STELLA's left cheek, caps the marker, and hands it to NANNETTE.)*

I'd suggest you get yourself a plastic nose, Stella.

MARION: And this is mine. *(She takes back her necklace.)*

> *(MARION puts the necklace on. HILARY, MARION, and NANNETTE stand. STELLA scrambles up and backs into a corner, staring at RITZ, DI, and JANEY, who avoid her eyes.)*

STELLA: What's with you guys? You lose your minds?

HILARY: *(To NANNETTE.)* Did you want to use the can? We'll back you.

NANNETTE: Maybe later, thanks.

> *(NANNETTE exits.)*

STELLA: *(To the Faces.)* Look at me. I said, look at me. What am I, invisible? Your ears don't work? This is an order. Look at me.

> *(The Faces avoid looking at STELLA. MARION edges toward the door.)*

HILARY: *(To MARION with mock sternness.)* Did you wash your hands?

MARION: Uh, later.

> *(MARION exits.)*

HILARY: Geez, what's the rush?

> *(HILARY grins at RITZ and DI, and starts to pull on her plastic nose set.)*

STELLA: All right, I'll do it myself.

> *(She pulls a switchblade and lunges at HILARY.)*

RITZ: No!

> *(Together RITZ and HILARY grab STELLA and remove the knife.)*

HILARY: The Code is dead.

STELLA: Don't listen to her, you guys. I'm always right, remember?

HILARY: *(To RITZ.)* You want this?

> *(RITZ accepts the knife. Then she reaches out slowly and touches HILARY's knife scar. The two girls lock eyes.)*

STELLA: Ritz, her face is garbage.

HILARY: *(To RITZ.)* Don't cut anyone who's down.

> *(HILARY and RITZ release STELLA who stands slumped. HILARY pulls her nose set on completely and pats it.)*

I'm outta here.

> *(HILARY turns to look one last time at STELLA, who avoids her eyes. HILARY exits.)*

STELLA: What's with you guys? Why didn't you back me up? When your leader calls, you're supposed to obey. We're together, we're the Faces.

> *(Without looking at her, RITZ and DI exit.)*

You like me, don't you, Janey? You still like me, you'll do what I say, won't you? I'm still your leader, I give the orders, I run this school with my little finger, don't I, Janey? Janey?

JANEY: See you 'round, I guess.

> *(JANEY exits. STELLA stands alone. She turns to the mirror and rubs the magic marker scar on her face, trying to remove it.)*

STELLA: Shit, you're ugly. You've always been ugly.

> *(She exits.)*

Scene Seventeen

> *(All cast members sit at their bedroom mirrors, holding unlit flashlights. The scene is dark. One by one, the teenagers turn on their flashlights. MARION, NANNETTE, KEVIN, and HILARY wear fake nose sets. STELLA worries the magic marker scar, trying to rub it off. There are soft sighs and groans. All cast members now have their flashlights on, studying their faces.)*

DARYL: God, I'm getting a zit.

RITZ: I have to get a nose job. I just have to get a nose job.

KEVIN: Terminal.

NANNETTE: *(Touching her nose set.)* You can only go so far with this.

MARION: It's like a new Code, really.

> *(Slowly HILARY removes her nose set and drops it on the floor. She begins to hum.)*

STELLA: Shit, you're ugly.

MARION: *(Looking around.)* I can hear singing.

KEVIN: Hey, sis!

NANNETTE: *(Looking around.)* Beautiful singing.

> *(HILARY runs her fingers over her face, claiming it. Then she turns off her flashlight.)*

HILARY: *(Singing.)*
It's dark now, I'm feeling my way.

JANEY: I'm afraid of the dark.

HILARY: *(Singing.)*
I've turned out the lights to meet this stranger.

DI: Be careful about strangers. Always be ready.

KEVIN: Keep singing, sis. I'm with you, I'm with you.

HILARY: *(Singing.)*
All my life my eyes couldn't see her
I've let the dark come, now I can feel her.

> *(KEVIN, NANNETTE, and MARION remove their plastic nose sets and turn out their flashlights.)*

NANNETTE: The Face is gone.

MARION: The Code is gone.

KEVIN: Feel.

HILARY: *(Singing.)*
Under my fingers, she starts to grow …

STELLA: Turn it off. Shut her up.

HILARY: *(Singing.)*
Where there was nothing, I can touch her song now …

JANEY: Can you stop my face from bleeding?

HILARY: *(Singing.)*
She's singing my blood, she's singing my bone …

> *(JANEY turns out her light.)*

She's singing my face, now I am home.

STELLA: Someone shut her up!

DARYL: *(To STELLA.)* Put a lid on it.

DI: Shh.

RITZ: Listen.

> *(DI, RITZ, and DARYL turn out their flashlights.)*

KEVIN: Keep singing, sis.

HILARY: *(Singing.)*
  The face is the place
  I flow like a river
  The face is the place
  I cry like the rain
  My face is my place
  My place to be free
  The place I belong to
  The stranger is me.

  (STELLA is now the only cast member with her flashlight on. She begins to gently touch her face, run her fingers across it.

  HILARY turns on her flashlight, lighting her own face.)

Welcome to the human face.

  (All cast members turn to face the audience and turn on their flashlights, lighting their own faces.)

ALL: *(Together.)* Face!

  (The end.)

Contributors

EDWARD ROY is an award-winning writer, director, actor, and the artistic director of Topological Theatre. Nominated for numerous Chalmers and Dora Awards for writing and directing, he received the Chalmers Playwriting Award for *A Secret Life* and Doras for his plays *The Other Side of the Closet* and *White Trash Blue Eyes*. He is also the recipient of the Pauline McGibbon Award for directing. His new play, *The Mother's Saint,* produced by Topological Theatre and Theatre Passe Muraille, Toronto, premièred in February 2000.

CARMEN AGUIRRE is a Chilean-born theatre artist who currently lives in Vancouver where she is director of The Latino Theatre Group. In addition to *Chile con Carne,* which has been produced to critical acclaim in Vancouver, Toronto, Chile, and Venezuela, she is the co-creator of *Dreams of Reality* with Sonia Norris and James Fagan Tait, based on *The Book of Embraces* by Eduardo Galeano, and *The Body says I am a Fiesta* with James Fagan Tait, based on *Walking Words* by Eduardo Galeano, both of which were produced at the Firehall Arts Centre, Vancouver. She is the author of *A Land Called I Don't Remember,* produced by Studio 58 in Vancouver, and *Maqui* and *Southern Cross,* produced by The Women in View Festival. She acts and directs and is currently writing *The Refugee Hotel,* a play based on the experiences of the first wave of Chilean refugees to arrive in Vancouver who were put up in a downtown hotel. *¿Que Pasa with La Raza, eh?,* also by Ms. Aguirre, is anthologized in *Along Human Lines: Dramas from Refugee Lives* (Blizzard).

BETH GOOBIE is the author of eleven books of fiction for young adults including *Mission Impossible* which was short-listed for the Governor General's Award for Children's Literature in 1995. She is also an award-winning poet, and the author of two collections of short fiction for adults. Her plays include *Continuum,* a radio play produced for CBC Radio's *Morningside, Dandelion Moon,* commissioned and produced by Catalyst Theatre in Edmonton, and *Janine Fowler Did It,* produced by the Guelph Collegiate Vocational Institute. *The Face is the Place* was originally commissioned and produced by the Guelph Collegiate Vocational Institute, Guelph in 1998.